Creative
Visualization

ALSO BY SHAKTI GAWAIN

BOOKS

Awakening
Creating True Prosperity
The Creative Visualization Workbook
Developing Intuition
The Four Levels of Healing
Living in the Light (with Laurel King)
The Living in the Light Workbook
Meditations
The Path of Transformation
Reflections in the Light
Return to the Garden

CDs

Creative Visualization
Creative Visualization Meditations
Meditations
Developing Intuition

GIFT

Create Your Own Affirmations Kit
The Creative Visualization Deck
The Developing Intuition Deck

THIRTIETH ANNIVERSARY EDITION

Creative Visualization

SHAKTI GAWAIN

Use the Power of Your
Imagination to Create What
You Want in Your Life

NATARAJ PUBLISHING

a division of

NEW WORLD LIBRARY
NOVATO, CALIFORNIA

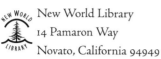 Nataraj Publishing

a division of

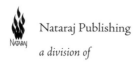 New World Library
14 Pamaron Way
Novato, California 94949

Copyright © 2002, 1995, 1978 by Shakti Gawain
Audio program ℗ 1996 New World Library
Creative Visualization® is a registered trademark of New World Library.

Design by Mary Ann Casler
Author photograph by Sumner Fowler
Audio program engineered by Janet Stark, Rampant Productions

Library of Congress Cataloging-in-Publication Data
Gawain, Shakti.
Creative visualization : use the power of your imagination to create what you want in your life / Shakti Gawain. — 30th anniversary ed., [2nd ed.].
    p.   cm.
ISBN 978-1-57731-636-7 (hardcover with slipcase and cd : alk. paper)
1. Visualization. 2. Affirmations. 3. Self-actualization (Psychology) I. Title.
BF367.G34 2008
153.3′2—dc22   2008014400

First printing of thirtieth anniversary edition, September 2008
ISBN 978-1-57731-636-7
Printed in China

 New World Library is a proud member of the Green Press Initiative.

10   9   8   7   6   5   4

This book is dedicated to you.

CONTENTS

PUBLISHER'S PREFACE

I met Shakti Gawain in Berkeley, California, in 1974, when we were both in our twenties. Shakti had just spent two years working her way around the world, traveling overland across Europe and Asia. She had spent several months in India, and her experiences there had a deep impact on her life. We quickly discovered we had a lot in common, including a deep dedication to personal development, a fascination with integrating the spiritual and psychological wisdom of East and West, and a strong desire to make a positive difference in the world.

In 1977, we co-wrote and published a little book called *Reunion: Tools for Transformation*. We had no capital and very little business experience, but after each small step we took, the next step became obvious. Looking back, it feels as if we were led by spirit every step of the way.

In 1978, Shakti wrote her first book, *Creative Visualization*. We initially printed two thousand copies of the book. We had to borrow money to pay the printing bill. I don't recall that we spent anything at all on promotion; I don't think we sent out even one review copy. But the print run sold out, quickly, purely by word of mouth. Booksellers kept telling us that people would come in, buy a copy, and return a few days later and want five or ten copies to give to their friends. The book initially sold itself — I'm sure it was because of Shakti's clear, beautiful writing as well as the solid content of the book. It was the kind of book people wanted to read and reread, the kind of book people kept in a special place and cherished for everything it had given them. It was the rare kind of book that helps people make wonderful changes in their lives.

We started to get deeply touching letters from readers very soon after publication. Each one had a story. Story after story began to pour in. One of my favorites summed up the feelings of many readers:

> Other self-help books I've read have made me feel as if someone was pointing a finger at me and telling me, "This is how it is!" But Shakti took me by the hand, led me into a beautiful garden, and handed me a bouquet of flowers, one at a time. Quietly, gently, and with great caring. Thank you for a beautiful book.

Creative Visualization has now sold more than six million copies — more than three million in North America, and at least another three million throughout the world in thirty-five foreign editions. It has proven to be a seminal work with global influence. The book launched Shakti's career as an internationally known and loved speaker and seminar leader, and it launched my career as a publisher as well. The book has shown us both how to visualize and create success, and I am eternally grateful that Shakti had the vision and courage to write it.

It is my hope and prayer that reading *Creative Visualization* will help you create exactly the kind of life you want, so that you're truly fulfilled, prosperous, healthy, and filled with creative energy. You hold in your hands a book that has helped a great many people improve the quality of their lives.

Marc Allen
June 2002

INTRODUCTION TO THE
REVISED EDITION

It's hard for me to believe that it has been so many years since *Creative Visualization* was first published.

At the time, I was thirty years old and just in the process of discovering my life's work. For a number of years I had been an active seeker, dedicating myself to exploring Eastern philosophy and Western psychology in an attempt to discover the deeper meaning and purpose of my life. Certain ideas and techniques I had learned were, in fact, having a profound effect on my awareness and my way of living.

I'm the kind of person who, once I discover something meaningful, simply can't help telling everyone who's willing to listen. So I found myself beginning to counsel people and lead small groups and workshops, teaching the concepts and exercises that were helping me solve my personal problems and expand my awareness.

It occurred to me that it might be a good idea to write these things down in a little book that I could make available to my students. As I was writing the book, I experienced alternating waves of creative enthusiasm and self-doubt, thinking, "Who am I to write a book telling people how to find greater happiness and fulfillment in life? I'm certainly no expert. My life isn't perfect."

My friend Marc Allen helped me get through the rough spots, encouraging me to stop worrying about it and just focus on my creative process. We decided to publish the book ourselves, even though we had very little knowledge of publishing and even less money. Somehow we managed to get the book out there in a few bookstores.

The rest is history. People seemed to love the book, and it sold by word of mouth. Gradually over the next few years it became a bestseller, and it continues to be very popular to this day, all over the world. I think one reason for its popularity is that it is short, simple, and practical and has techniques that readers can begin using immediately and effectively.

It has been extremely satisfying to receive thousands of letters telling me how much this book has helped people with specific and sometimes serious problems. I am grateful to have been given the opportunity to contribute in this way.

My work has blossomed right along with the book. For many years I have been leading workshops all over the world, and I have written and published several other books. *Creative Visualization* helped me find my path in life, just as it has helped others.

The time has come for a new revised edition. I have made relatively few changes, simply trying to clarify certain points, deepen certain concepts, and generally update it.

If you are already familiar with the first edition, I hope you enjoy the changes. If this is your first experience with *Creative Visualization*, may it help you create all that your heart and soul desire.

Shakti Gawain

May 2002

A LETTER TO MY READERS

D ear Friends,

    I decided to write this book because it seemed like the best way I could think of to share with others the many wonderful things I have learned that have so deepened and expanded my experience and enjoyment of life.

I do not consider myself by any means an expert on the art of creative visualization. I am a student of the subject, and the more I study and use creative visualization myself, the more I discover how vast and deep its potential is . . . truly it is as infinitely creative as your own imagination.

This book is meant as an introduction and workbook for learning and using creative visualization. Very little of the material is original to me; it is a synthesis of the most practical and useful ideas and techniques that I've learned in my personal study.

My sources are many. I've included at the end a list of recommended resources that I think you will find interesting and helpful.

This book contains many different techniques. You will probably find that it works best not to try to absorb them all at once, but more gradually. I suggest that you read the book slowly, trying some of the exercises as you go along, and giving yourself the chance to absorb them deeply. Or you might want to read it once through, then reread it more slowly.

This book is my gift to you in love ... may it be a blessing to you ... may it help you bring more and more joy, satisfaction, and beauty into your life ... may it nurture the light that is shining within you. . . .

Enjoy!

With love,

Shakti

PART ONE

Basics of Creative Visualization

Every moment of your life is infinitely creative
and the universe is endlessly bountiful.
Just put forth a clear enough request,
and everything your heart truly desires must come to you.

WHAT IS
CREATIVE VISUALIZATION?

Creative visualization is the technique of using your imagination to create what you want in your life. There is nothing at all new, strange, or unusual about creative visualization. You are already using it every day, every minute, in fact. It is your natural power of imagination, the basic creative energy of the universe, which you use constantly, whether or not you are aware of it.

In the past, many of us have used our power of creative visualization in a relatively unconscious way. Because of our own deep-seated negative concepts about life, we have automatically and unconsciously expected and imagined lack, limitation, difficulties, and problems to be our lot in life. To one degree or another that is what we have created for ourselves.

This book is about learning to use your natural creative imagination in a more and more conscious way, as a technique to create what you *truly* want — love, fulfillment, enjoyment, satisfying relationships, rewarding work, self-expression, health, beauty, prosperity, inner peace, and harmony…whatever your heart desires. The use of creative visualization gives us a key to tap into the natural goodness and bounty of life.

Imagination is the ability to create an idea, a mental picture, or a feeling sense of something. In creative visualization you use your imagination to create a clear image, idea, or feeling of something you wish to manifest. Then you continue to focus on the idea, feeling, or picture regularly, giving it positive energy until it becomes objective reality…in other words, until you actually achieve what you have been imagining.

Your goal may be on any level — physical, emotional, mental, or spiritual. You might imagine yourself with a new home, or with a new job, or having a satisfying relationship, or feeling calm and serene, or perhaps with an improved memory and learning ability. Or you might picture yourself handling a difficult situation effortlessly, or simply see yourself as a radiant being, filled with life energy. You can work on any level, and all will have results…through experience you will find the particular images and techniques that work best for you.

Let us say, for example, that you are feeling unsatisfied in your current job situation. If you feel that the job is basically right for you but there are factors that need improvement, you could begin by imagining the improvements that you desire. If that doesn't work, or if you feel that you would prefer a new job, then focus on imagining yourself in the employment situation that you desire.

Either way, the technique is basically the same. After relaxing into a deep, quiet, meditative state of mind, imagine that you are working in your ideal job situation. Imagine yourself in the physical setting or environment that you would like, doing work that you enjoy and find satisfying, interacting with people in a harmonious way, receiving appreciation and appropriate financial compensation. Add any other details that are important for you, such as the hours you work, the amount of autonomy and/or responsibility you have, and so on. Try to get a feeling in yourself that this is possible; experience it as if it were already happening. In short, imagine it exactly the way you'd like it to be, as if it were already so!

Repeat this short, simple exercise often, perhaps twice a day, or whenever you think about it. If your desire and intention to make a change are clear, chances are good that you may find some type of shift taking place in your work, fairly soon.

It should be noted here that this technique *cannot* be used to "control" the behavior of others or cause them to do something against their will. Its effect is to dissolve our internal barriers to natural harmony and self-realization, allowing everyone to manifest in his or her most positive aspect.

5

To use creative visualization it is not necessary to believe in any metaphysical or spiritual ideas, though you must be willing to entertain certain concepts as being possible. It is not necessary to "have faith" in any power outside yourself.

The only thing necessary is that you have the desire to enrich your knowledge and experience, and an open enough mind to try something new in a positive spirit.

Study the principles, try the techniques with an open mind and heart, and then judge for yourself whether they are useful to you.

If so, continue using and developing them, and soon the changes in yourself and your life will probably exceed anything you could have originally dreamed of....

Creative visualization is magic in the truest and highest meaning of the word. It involves understanding and aligning yourself with the natural principles that govern the workings of our universe, and learning to use these principles in the most conscious and creative way.

If you had never seen a gorgeous flower or a spectacular sunset before, and someone described one to you, you might consider it to be a miraculous thing (which it truly is!). Once you saw a few yourself, and began to learn something about the natural laws involved, you would begin to understand how they are formed, and it would seem natural to you and not particularly mysterious.

The same is true of the process of creative visualization. What at first might seem amazing or impossible to the very limited type of education our rational minds have received, becomes perfectly understandable once we learn, and practice with, the underlying concepts involved.

Once you do so, it may seem that you are working miracles in your life ... and you truly will be!

HOW CREATIVE
VISUALIZATION WORKS

In order to understand how creative visualization works, it's useful to look at several interrelated principles:

THE PHYSICAL UNIVERSE IS ENERGY

The scientific world is beginning to discover what metaphysical and spiritual teachers have known for centuries. Our physical universe is not really composed of any "matter" at all; its basic component is a kind of force or essence that we call *energy*.

Things appear to be solid and separate from one another on the level at which our physical senses normally perceive them. On finer levels, however, atomic and subatomic levels, seemingly solid matter is seen as smaller and smaller particles within particles, which eventually turn out to be just pure energy.

Physically, we are all energy, and everything within and around us is made up of energy. We are all part of one great energy field.

Things that we perceive to be solid and separate are in reality just various forms of our essential energy which is common to all. We are all one, even in a literal, physical sense.

The energy is vibrating at different rates of speed, and thus has different qualities, from finer to denser. Thought is a relatively fine, light form of energy and, therefore, very quick and easy to change. Matter is relatively dense, compact energy and, therefore, slower to move and change. Within matter there is great variation as well. Living flesh is relatively fine, changes quickly, and is easily affected by many things. A rock is a much denser form, slower to change, and more difficult to affect. Yet even rock is eventually changed and affected by the fine, light energy of water, for example. All forms of energy are interrelated and can affect one another.

ENERGY IS MAGNETIC

One law of energy is this: Energy of a certain quality or vibration tends to attract energy of a similar quality and vibration.

Thoughts and feelings have their own magnetic energy that attracts energy of a similar nature. We can see this principle at work, for instance, when we "accidentally" run into someone we've just been thinking of, or "happen" to pick up a book that contains exactly the perfect information we need at that moment.

FORM FOLLOWS IDEA

Thought is a quick, light, mobile form of energy. It manifests instantaneously, unlike the denser forms such as matter.

When we create something, we always create it first in thought form. A thought or idea always precedes manifestation. "I think I'll make dinner" is the idea that precedes creation of a meal. "I want a new dress" precedes going and buying one; "I need a job" precedes finding one, and so on.

An artist first has an idea or inspiration, then creates a painting. A builder first has a design, then builds a house.

The idea is like a blueprint; it creates an image of the form, which then magnetizes and guides the physical energy to flow into that form, and eventually manifests it on the physical plane.

The same principle holds true even if we do not take direct physical action to manifest our ideas. Simply having an idea or thought, holding it in your mind, is an energy that will tend to attract and create that form on the material plane. If you constantly think of illness, you may eventually become ill; if you believe yourself to be beautiful, you become so. Unconscious ideas and feelings held inside of us operate in the same way.

9

THE LAW OF RADIATION AND ATTRACTION

This is the principle that whatever you put out into the universe will be reflected back to you. "As you sow, so shall you reap."

What this means from a practical standpoint is that we always attract into our lives whatever we think about the most, believe in most strongly, expect on the deepest levels, and/or imagine most vividly.

When we are negative and fearful, insecure or anxious, we often attract the very experiences, situations, or people that we are seeking to avoid. If we are basically positive in attitude, expecting and envisioning pleasure, satisfaction, and happiness, we tend to attract and create people, situations, and events that conform to our positive expectations. So, consciously imagining what we want can help us to manifest it in our lives.

USING CREATIVE VISUALIZATION

The process of change does not occur on superficial levels, through mere "positive thinking." It involves exploring, discovering, and changing our deepest, most basic *attitudes toward life*. That is why learning to use creative visualization can become an experience of deep and meaningful growth. In the process we often discover ways in which we have been holding ourselves back, blocking ourselves from achieving satisfaction and fulfillment in our lives through our fears and unconscious beliefs. Once seen clearly, these limiting attitudes can often be dissolved through the creative visualization process, leaving space for us to find and live a natural state of greater happiness, fulfillment, and love. . . .

At first you may practice creative visualization at specific times and for specific goals. As you get more in the habit of using it, and begin to trust the results it can bring you, you will find that it becomes an integral part of your thinking process. It becomes a continuous awareness, a state of consciousness in which you know that you are the constant creator of your life.

That is the ultimate point of creative visualization — to make every moment of our lives a moment of wondrous creation, in which we are just naturally choosing the best, the most beautiful, the most fulfilling lives we can imagine. . . .

A SIMPLE EXERCISE
IN CREATIVE VISUALIZATION

Here is an exercise in the basic technique of creative visualization:

First, think of something you would like. For this exercise choose something simple, something that you can easily imagine attaining. It might be an object you would like to have, an event you would like to have happen, a situation in which you'd like to find yourself, or some circumstance in your life you'd like to improve.

Get in a comfortable position, either sitting or lying down, in a quiet place where you won't be disturbed. Relax your body completely. Starting from your toes and moving up to your scalp, think of relaxing each muscle in your body in turn, letting all tension flow out of your body. Breathe deeply and slowly, from your belly. Count down slowly from ten to one, feeling yourself getting more deeply relaxed with each count.

When you feel deeply relaxed, start to imagine the thing you want exactly as you would like it. If it is an object, imagine yourself with the object, using it, admiring it, enjoying it, showing it to friends. If it is a situation or event, imagine yourself there and everything happening just as you want it to. You may imagine what people are saying, or any details that make it more real to you.

You may take a relatively short time or quite a few minutes to imagine this — whatever feels best to you. Have fun with it. It should be a thoroughly enjoyable experience, like a child daydreaming about what he wants for his birthday.*

Now, keeping the idea or image still in your mind, mentally make some very positive, affirmative statements to yourself (aloud or silently, as you prefer) about it, such as:

Here I am spending a wonderful weekend in the mountains. What a beautiful vacation.

or

I love the view from my spacious, new apartment.

or

I'm learning to love and accept myself as I am.

These positive statements, called affirmations, are a very important part of creative visualization, which I discuss in more detail later.

If you like, you can end your visualization with the firm statement to yourself:

---

* To avoid the awkwardness of saying "his or her" constantly, I have sometimes used the masculine pronoun and sometimes the feminine. Obviously, any exercise in this book is appropriate for either sex.

This, or something better,
now manifests for me
in totally satisfying and harmonious ways,
for the highest good of all concerned.

This statement leaves room for something different and even better than you had originally envisioned happening, and serves as a reminder to you that this process only functions for the mutual benefit of all.

If doubts or contradictory thoughts arise, don't resist them or try to prevent them. This will tend to give them a power they don't otherwise have. Just let them flow through your consciousness, acknowledge them, and return to your positive statements and images.

Do this process only as long as you find it enjoyable and interesting. It could be five minutes or half an hour. Repeat every day, or as often as you can.

As you see, the basic process is relatively simple. Using it really effectively, however, usually requires some understanding and refinement.

IT'S IMPORTANT TO RELAX

It's important to relax deeply when you are first learning to use creative visualization. When your body and mind are deeply relaxed, your brain wave pattern actually changes and becomes slower. This deeper, slower level is commonly called the alpha level (while your usual busy waking consciousness is called the beta level), and much research is being done on its effects.

The alpha level has been found to be a very healthful state of consciousness, because of its relaxing effect on mind and body. And, interestingly enough, it has been found to be far more effective than the more active beta level in creating real changes in the so-called objective world, through the use of visualization. What this means for our practical purposes is that if you learn to relax deeply and do creative visualization, you may be able to make far more effective changes in your life than you would by thinking, worrying, planning, and trying to manipulate things and people.

If you have any particular way that you are accustomed to

relaxing deeply or entering a quiet, meditative state, by all means use that method. Otherwise you may wish to continue using the method I describe in the previous chapter — breathing slowly and deeply, relaxing each muscle in your body in turn, and counting down from ten to one slowly. If you have any trouble physically relaxing, you might want to seek instruction in yoga, meditation, or stress reduction, which will be helpful in this regard. Of course, a side benefit of all of this is that you will find deep relaxation healthful and beneficial mentally, emotionally, and physically.

It is especially good to do creative visualization at night just before sleeping, or in the morning just after awakening, because at those times the mind and body are already deeply relaxed and receptive. You might like to do it while lying in bed, but if you tend to fall asleep, it's best to sit up on the edge of the bed or in a chair in a comfortable position, with your spine straight and balanced. Having your spine straight helps the energy flow and makes it easier to get a deep alpha wave pattern.

If it's possible for you, a short period of meditation and creative visualization done at midday will relax and renew you, and cause your day to flow more smoothly.

HOW TO VISUALIZE

Many people wonder exactly what is meant by the term "visualize." Some worry because they don't actually "see" a mental picture or image when they close their eyes and try to visualize. When some people first try to visualize, they feel that "nothing is happening." Usually, they are simply blocking themselves by trying too hard. They may be feeling that there's a "right way" to do this, and that their own experience is incorrect or inadequate. If this is how you feel, you need to stop worrying, relax, and accept what happens naturally for you.

Don't get stuck on the term "visualize." *It is not at all necessary to mentally see an image.* Some people say they see very clear, sharp images when they close their eyes and imagine something. Others don't really "see" anything; they sense or feel it, or they just sort of "think about" it. That's perfectly fine. Some people are more visually oriented, some are auditory, others are more kinesthetic. We all use our imaginations constantly — it's impossible not to, so whatever process you find yourself doing when you imagine is fine.

If you still don't feel sure what it means to visualize, read through each of these exercises, then close your eyes and see what comes naturally to you:

Close your eyes and relax deeply. Think of some familiar room, such as your bedroom or living room. Remember some familiar details of it, such as the color of the carpet, the way the furniture is arranged, how bright or dark it is. Imagine yourself walking into the room and sitting or lying down on a comfortable chair, couch, or bed.

Now recall some pleasant experience you have had in the last few days, especially one involving good physical sensations, such as eating a delicious meal, receiving a massage, swimming in cool water, or making love. Remember the experience as vividly as possible, and enjoy the pleasurable sensations once again.

Now imagine that you are in some idyllic country setting, perhaps relaxing on soft green grass beside a cool river, or wandering through a beautiful, lush forest. It can be a place that you have been, or an ideal place where you would like to go. Think of the details, and create it any way you would like it to be.

Whatever process you used to bring these scenes to your mind is your way of "visualizing."

There are actually two different modes involved in creative visualization. One is receptive, the other is active. In the receptive mode we simply relax and allow images or impressions to come to us without choosing the details of them; we take what comes. In the active mode we consciously choose and create what we wish to see or imagine. Both these processes are an important part of creative visualization, and both your receptive and active abilities will be strengthened through practice.

SPECIAL PROBLEMS WITH VISUALIZATION

Occasionally a person has completely blocked his ability to visualize or imagine at will, and feels that he simply "can't do it." This type of block usually arises from a fear, and it can be worked through if the person who experiences the difficulty desires to solve the problem.

Usually a person blocks his ability to use creative visualization out of a fear of what he may encounter by looking inside himself — fear of his own unacknowledged feelings and emotions.

For example, a man in one of my classes was consistently unable to visualize, and kept falling asleep during the meditations. It turned out that he had once had a profoundly emotional experience during a visualization process, and he was afraid he would be embarrassed by becoming emotional in front of others.

A woman client of mine had difficulty visualizing until she went through therapy and was able to get in touch with, experience, and release painful feelings that she had buried inside since childhood.

The truth is that there is *nothing* within us that can hurt us; it is only our fear of experiencing our own feelings that can keep us trapped.

If anything unusual or unexpected arises during meditation, the best thing is simply to look at it fully, be with it, and experience it as much as you can, and you will find that it, eventually will lose any negative power over you. Our fears arise from things we don't confront. Once we are willing to look fully and *deeply* at the source of a fear, it loses its power. If we feel overwhelmed, it can be very helpful to get support from a good counselor or therapist who can help us accept and express our feelings. This is especially important if we've had a lot of pain or trauma in our lives.

19

Fortunately, problems with visualization are relatively rare. As a rule, creative visualization comes naturally, and the more you practice it, the easier it becomes. If visualization is difficult for you, you may find that saying affirmations is easier and more effective (see later chapters).

FOUR BASIC STEPS FOR EFFECTIVE CREATIVE VISUALIZATION

1. SET YOUR GOAL

Decide on something you would like to have, work toward, realize, or create. It can be on any level — a job, a house, a relationship, a change in yourself, increased prosperity, a happier state of mind, improved health, beauty, a better physical condition, solving a problem in your family or community, or whatever.

At first, choose goals that are fairly easy for you to believe in, that you feel are possible to realize in the fairly near future. That way you won't have to deal with too much negative resistance in yourself, and you can maximize your feelings of success as you are learning creative visualization. Later, when you have more practice, you can take on more difficult or challenging problems and issues.

2. CREATE A CLEAR IDEA OR PICTURE

Create an idea, a mental picture, or a feeling of the object or situation exactly as you want it. You should think of it in the present tense as already existing the way you want it to be. Imagine yourself in the situation as you desire it, now. Include as many details as you can.

You may wish to make an actual physical picture of it as well, by making a treasure map (described in detail later). This is an optional step, not at all necessary, but often helpful (and fun!).

3. FOCUS ON IT OFTEN

Bring your idea or mental picture to mind often, both in quiet meditation periods, and also casually throughout the day, when you happen to think of it. In this way it becomes an integrated part of your life, and it becomes more of a reality for you.

Focus on it clearly, yet in a light, relaxed way. It's important not to feel like you are striving too hard for it or putting an excessive amount of energy into it — that tends to hinder rather than help.

4. GIVE IT POSITIVE ENERGY

As you focus on your goal, think about it in a positive, encouraging way. Make strong positive statements to yourself: that it exists; that it has come or is now coming to you. See yourself receiving or achieving it. These positive statements are called "affirmations."* While you

---

* Affirmations are explained in more detail beginning on page 27.

use affirmations, try to temporarily suspend any doubts or disbelief you may have, at least for the moment, and practice getting the feeling that what you desire is very real and possible.

Continue to work with this process until you achieve your goal, or no longer have the desire to do so. Remember that goals often change before they are realized, which is a perfectly natural part of the human process of change and growth. So don't try to prolong it any longer than you have energy for it — if you lose interest it may mean that it's time for a new look at what you want.

If you find that a goal has changed for you, be sure to acknowledge that to yourself. Get clear in your mind the fact that you are no longer focusing on your previous goal. End the cycle of the old, and begin the cycle of the new. This helps you avoid getting confused, or feeling that you've "failed" when you have simply changed.

When you achieve a goal, be sure to acknowledge consciously to yourself that it has been completed. Often we achieve things that we have been desiring and visualizing, and we forget to even notice that we have succeeded! So give yourself some appreciation and a pat on the back, and be sure to thank the universe for fulfilling your requests.

23

CREATIVE VISUALIZATION
WORKS ONLY FOR GOOD

Don't fear that the power of creative visualization can be used for harmful ends. Creative visualization is a means of unblocking or dissolving the barriers we ourselves have created to the naturally harmonious, abundant, and loving flow of the universe. It is only truly effective when it is used in alignment with our highest goals and purposes, for the highest good of all beings.

If someone should attempt to use this powerful technique for a harmful or destructively selfish end, that person would only be demonstrating his or her ignorance of the law of karma. This is the same basic principle as the law of radiation and attraction, "As you sow, so shall you reap." Whatever you try to create for another will always boomerang back to you. That includes both loving, helpful, or healing actions and negative, destructive ones. This means, of course, that the more you use creative visualization to love and serve others' as well as your own highest ends, the more love, happiness, and success will just naturally find their way to you.

Just to make sure that you are aware of this, it's a good idea to add the following phrase to any creative visualization process you do:

This, or something better,
now manifests for me
in totally satisfying and harmonious ways,
for the highest good of all concerned.

As an example, if you are visualizing getting a job promotion, don't envision the person above you being fired, but imagine him or her moving on to other, better things or a better, more fulfilling job, so that it works out for the good of all. You don't need to understand or figure out how that will happen, or try to decide what is the best way it could work out; simply assume that it is working out for the best, and let universal intelligence take care of the details.

AFFIRMATIONS

Affirmations are one of the most important elements of creative visualization. To affirm means "to make firm." An affirmation is a strong, positive statement that something is *already* so. It is a way of "making firm" that which you are imaging.

Most of us are aware of the fact that we have a nearly continuous inner "dialogue" going on in our minds. The mind is busy "talking" to itself, keeping up an endless commentary about life, the world, our feelings, our problems, and other people.

The words and ideas that run through our minds are very important. Most of the time we aren't consciously aware of this stream of thoughts, and yet what we are "telling ourselves" in our minds is the basis on which we form our experience of reality. Our mental commentary influences and colors our feelings and perceptions about what's going on in our lives, and it is these thought forms that ultimately attract and create everything that happens to us.

Anyone who has practiced meditation knows how difficult

it can be to quiet this inner "mind talk," in order to connect with our deeper, wiser intuitive mind. One traditional meditation practice involves simply observing the inner dialogue as objectively as possible.

This is a very valuable experience, as it allows you to become consciously aware of the content of your thoughts. Many of these thoughts are like tape recordings of old patterns we've had all our lives. They are old "programming" we picked up long ago, which is still influencing what's happening to us today. For example, we might find that we habitually think self-defeating thoughts such as, "I'm not going to be able to do this," or "This is never going to work out right."

The practice of engaging in affirmations allows us to begin replacing some of our stale, worn out, or negative mind chatter with more positive ideas and concepts. It is a powerful technique, one that can in a short time transform many of our attitudes and expectations about life, and thereby help to change what we create for ourselves.

Affirmations can be done silently, spoken aloud, written down, or even sung or chanted. Even ten minutes a day of repeating effective affirmations can counterbalance years of old mental habits. If you become aware that you are repeating habitual negative thought patterns or attitudes, try saying an affirmation to yourself a few times right then and there.

For example, if you find yourself thinking, "Oh, what's the use; I'll never get what I want," you might say to yourself, "I have the ability to create what I want in my life," or "I deserve to be happy and fulfilled."

An affirmation can be any positive statement. It can be very general or very specific. There are an infinite number of possible affirmations; here are a few, just to give you some ideas:

Every day, in every way, I'm getting better and better.

Everything I need is coming to me easily and effortlessly.

My life is blossoming in total perfection.

I have everything I need to enjoy my here and now.

I am the master of my life.

Everything I need is already within me.

Perfect wisdom is in my heart.

I am whole and complete in myself.

I love and appreciate myself just as I am.

I accept all my feelings as part of me.

I love to love and be loved.

The more I love myself, the more love I have to give others.

I now give and receive love freely.

*I am now attracting loving, satisfying relationships
into my life.*

*My relationship with _____ is growing
happier and more fulfilling every day.*

I now have a satisfying, well-paying job.

*I love doing my work, and I am richly rewarded,
creatively and financially.*

I am an open channel of creative energy.

I am dynamically self-expressive.

I enjoy relaxing and having fun.

I communicate clearly and effectively.

It's okay for me to have everything I want!

*I now have enough time, energy, wisdom,
and money to accomplish all my desires.*

*I am always in the right place at the right time,
successfully engaged in the right activity.*

*This is an abundant universe and there's plenty
for all of us.*

Abundance is my natural state of being.

Every day I am growing more financially prosperous.

The more I have, the more I have to give.

The more I give, the more I receive, and the happier I feel.

It's okay for me to have fun and enjoy myself, and I do!

*I am relaxed and centered. I have plenty of time
for everything.*

I am now enjoying everything I do.

I feel happy just being alive.

I am healthy and beautiful!

*I am open to receiving all the blessings
of this abundant universe!*

_____ is coming to me, easily and effortlessly.

I have a wonderful job with wonderful pay.

I do a wonderful service in a wonderful way.

*The light within me is creating miracles in my life
here and now.*

All things are now working together for good in my life.

I am now attuned to my higher purpose in life.

*I now recognize, accept, and follow the divine plan of my life as it is
revealed to me step by step.*

I give thanks now for my life of health, happiness,
and self-expression.

Here are some important things to remember about affirmations:

1. Always phrase affirmations in the present tense, not in
    the future. It's important to create your desire as if it
    already exists. Don't say, "I will get a wonderful new job,"
    but rather, "I now have a wonderful new job." This is
    not lying to yourself; it is acknowledging the fact that
    everything is created *first* on the inner plane, before it
    can manifest in external reality.

2. Always phrase affirmations in the most positive way you
    can. Affirm what you *do* want, not what you *don't* want.
    Don't say, "I no longer oversleep in the morning," but
    rather, "I now wake up on time and full of energy in the
    morning." This ensures that you are creating the most
    positive possible mental image.

    At certain times you may find it helpful to phrase
    affirmations negatively, especially when you are working
    on clearing out specific emotional blocks or bad habits,
    such as, "I don't need to get tense in order to get things
    accomplished." If so, you should *always follow* this type of
    affirmation with a positive one that describes what you
    desire to create, such as, "I now stay deeply relaxed and
    centered, and everything is accomplished easily and
    effortlessly."

3. In general, the shorter and simpler the affirmation, the
    more effective. An affirmation should be a clear state-
    ment that conveys a strong feeling; the more feeling it

conveys, the stronger impression it makes on your mind. Affirmations that are long, wordy, and theoretical lose their emotional impact and become too mental.

4. Always choose affirmations that feel totally right for you. What works for one person may not work at all for another. An affirmation should feel positive, expansive, freeing, and/or supportive. If it doesn't, find another one, or try changing the words until it feels right.

    Of course, you may feel emotional resistance to any affirmation when you first use it, especially one that is really powerful for you and is going to make a real change in your consciousness. That is simply our natural fear of change and growth.

5. Always remember that you are creating something new and fresh. You are not trying to redo or change what already exists. To do so would be to resist what is, which creates conflict and struggle. Take the attitude that you are accepting and handling whatever already exists in your life, and at the same time taking every moment as a new opportunity to begin creating exactly what you desire and will make you happiest.

6. Affirmations are not meant to contradict or change your feelings or emotions. It is important to accept and experience all your feelings, including so-called negative ones, without attempting to change them. At the same time, affirmations can help you create a new point of view about life that will enable you to have more and more satisfying experiences from now on.

7. Try as much as possible to create a feeling of belief, and experience that your affirmations can be true. Temporarily (at least for a few minutes) suspend your doubts and hesitations, and put your full mental and emotional energy into them.

If doubts, resistance, or negative thoughts are getting in the way of doing your affirmations, do one of the clearing processes or the writing affirmations process given in Part Four of this book.

Rather than saying affirmations by rote, try to get the feeling that you really have the power to create that reality (which in fact you do!). This will make a big difference in how effective they are.

Affirmations can be used alone, or in combination with visualizing or imaging. It's very effective to include affirmations as part of your regular creative visualization meditation periods. Later in the book I give you ideas for many other ways to use affirmations.

For many people, affirmations are most powerful and inspiring when they include references to a spiritual source. Mention of God, the Goddess, the universe, a higher power, spirit, the Earth Mother, divine love, or whatever phrase you prefer adds spiritual energy to your affirmation and acknowledges the universal source of all things.

Here are some examples:

*I have the infinite creative power of the Goddess
within me.*

Divine love is working through me here and now to create this.

The Christ within me is creating miracles in my life here and now.

I am one with the Great Spirit.

My higher self is guiding me in everything that I do.

*God lives within me and manifests in the world
through me.*

*I give thanks to Mother Earth for nurturing and
sustaining me every day.*

*The light of God surrounds me, the love of God enfolds me, the power of
God flows through me. Wherever I am, God is, and all is well!*

A SPIRITUAL "PARADOX"

Sometimes people who have studied Eastern philosophy or are on a certain spiritual path feel a hesitation about using creative visualization when they first hear of it. Their conflict comes from the *apparent* paradox they see between the idea of "being here now," letting go of attachments and desires, and the idea of setting goals and creating what you want in life. I say *apparent* paradox because, in actuality, there is no contradiction between the two teachings when they are understood on a deeper level. They are both important principles that must be understood and lived in order for you to become a conscious person. In order to explain how they fit together, allow me to share with you my viewpoint about the process of inner growth.

Most people in our culture have become cut off from their awareness of their spiritual essence. We have temporarily lost our conscious connection with our souls and, thus, have lost our own sense of power and responsibility for our lives. In some inner way, we have a sense of helplessness; we feel basically powerless to make real change in our lives or in the world. This inner feeling of powerlessness causes us to overcompensate by striving and struggling very hard to have *some* degree of power or control in our world.

Most of us, therefore, become very goal oriented; we become emotionally attached to things and people outside of ourselves that we feel we need in order to be happy. We feel there is something "missing" inside ourselves, and we become tense, anxious, and stressed, continuously trying to fill up the gap, trying to manipulate the outside world in order to get what we want.

This is the state of being from which most of us are setting goals and trying to create what we want in life, and unfortunately, from this level of consciousness, it doesn't work at all... either we set up so many obstacles for ourselves that we *can't* succeed, or we *do* succeed in reaching our goals only to find that they don't bring us inner happiness.

It is at the point where we realize this dilemma that we begin to open up to a spiritual path. We realize that there simply has to be something more to life, and we begin to search for it.

We may go through many different experiences and processes on our search, but eventually we are gradually restored to ourselves. That is, we come back into an experience of our spiritual essence, the universal energy within us all. Through this experience we can be restored to our spiritual power, and the emptiness inside us is filled up *from within*.

Now to get back to our supposed paradox.

When we are coming out of the empty, grasping, manipulative condition, the first and foremost lesson to be learned is just to *let go*. We must relax, stop struggling, stop trying so hard, stop manipulating things and people to try to get what we want and need; in fact, stop *doing* so much and have an experience of just *being* for a while.

When we do this, we suddenly discover that we're really perfectly okay; in fact, we feel quite wonderful, just letting ourselves be, and letting the world be, without trying to change things. This is the basic experience of *being here now*, and it's what the Buddhist philosophy means by "letting go of attachment." It's similar to the Christian concept, "God's will be done." It's a very freeing experience, and a most basic one on any path of self-awareness.

Once you have begun to have this experience more and more often, you are opening up the channel to your soul, and sooner or later a great deal of natural creative energy will begin to flow through you. You start to see that you yourself are already creating your whole life and every experience that happens to you, and you become interested in creating more rewarding experiences for yourself and others. You begin to want to focus your energy toward the highest and most fulfilling goals that are real for you at any given moment. You realize that life can be basically good, abundant, and often fun, and that having what you truly want, without struggle and strain, is part of your natural birthright as a function of just being alive. This is the time when creative visualization can become a most important tool.

Here is a metaphor that I hope will make it even clearer:

Let us imagine that life is a river. Most people are clinging to the bank, afraid to let go and risk being carried along by the current of the river. At a certain point, each of us must be willing to simply let go, and trust the river to carry us along safely. At this point, we learn to "go with the flow" — and it feels wonderful.

Once we have become accustomed to being in the flow of the river, we can begin to look ahead and guide our course onward, deciding where the course looks best, steering the way around boulders and snags, and choosing which of the many channels and branches of the river we prefer to follow, all the while still "going with the flow."

This metaphor shows us how we can accept our lives here and now, flowing with what is, and at the same time guiding ourselves consciously toward our goals by taking responsibility for creating our own lives.

Remember, too, that creative visualization is a tool that can be used for any purpose, including one's own spiritual growth. It is often very helpful to use creative visualization in picturing yourself as a more relaxed, open person, flowing, living in the here and now, and always connected with your inner essence

May you be blessed
with everything
your heart desires.

PART TWO

Using Creative Visualization

Ask, and it shall be given you;
seek, and ye shall find;
knock, and it shall be opened unto you.
For every one that asketh, receiveth;
and he that seeketh, findeth;
and to him that knocketh it shall be opened.

— Matthew 7:7–8

MAKING CREATIVE VISUALIZATION
PART OF YOUR LIFE

As you can see from Part One, the basic technique of creative visualization is not difficult. The important thing now is to learn to use it in a way that really works for you...that helps you to make positive change in your life. In order to use creative visualization most effectively, it's helpful to understand certain concepts and learn some further techniques.

The most important thing to remember is to use creative visualization often, to make it a regular part of your life. Most people seem to find that it works best to practice it at least a little every day, especially when they are first learning.

I suggest that you have a regular creative visualization meditation period for fifteen minutes or so each morning when you wake up, and each evening before sleeping (these are the times when it is most effective), as well as the middle of the day if you can manage that. Always start your meditation periods with deep relaxation, then follow with any visualizations or affirmations you wish.

There are many different ways that creative visualization can be used, and it's up to you to remember to try them at appropriate times. Conscious creative visualization may mean a new way of thinking and a new way of living. As such, it will take some practice.

Try it out in different situations and under different circumstances, and use it as often as you can for any type of problem solving. If you find yourself worried or puzzled about anything, or feeling discouraged or frustrated about a problem, ask yourself if there is a way you could use creative visualization to help you. Form a creative habit of using it at every appropriate moment.

Don't get discouraged if you don't *immediately* feel totally successful with your creative visualization. Remember that most of us have years of negative thought patterns to overcome. It takes time to change some of these lifelong habits. And many of us have some underlying feelings and attitudes that can slow us down in our efforts to live more consciously.

42

Fortunately, creative visualization is such an innately powerful process that even five minutes of conscious, positive meditation can balance out hours, days, even years of negative patterns.

So be patient. It has taken a lifetime to create your world the way it is now. It may not necessarily change instantly. With perseverance and a proper understanding of the process, you will succeed in creating what seem like many miracles in your life.

Two things I have found most important in my growth process with creative visualization are:

1. Regular reading of inspiring and supportive books that help to keep me in touch with my highest ideals and aspirations and/or that can give me encouragement through difficult times. I usually keep a book by my bed and read a page or two each day.

2. Having a friend or (ideally) a community of friends who are also tuned into learning to live more consciously and who will support you and help you in your efforts. Attending regular or occasional consciousness classes or workshops, support groups or therapy, can be an important way of getting this type of support, and giving it to others as well.

In the following chapters I give you many different techniques, ideas, exercises, and meditations. Choose the ones that feel right to you and seem to work for you. There are many different levels and approaches to the creative visualization process, and I have tried to include a wide variety of possible practices. In any given situation, one may be appropriate and another may not. Follow the flow of your own energy, and use the ones that you feel drawn to.

For example, in a certain situation you may try to do affirmations and find that you simply can't repeat them, or you don't feel they are accomplishing anything. In that case you might want to try a clearing process, or get in touch with your inner guidance and ask for clarification, or just let go for a while and focus on other things.

What works at one time may not at another; what works for one person may not for another. Always trust yourself and your own deepest intuitive feelings.

If it feels like you are forcing, pushing, exerting effort, or straining, don't do it.

If it feels helpful, releasing, opening, strengthening, enlivening, or inspiring, do it.

43

BEING, DOING, AND HAVING

We can think of life as containing three aspects, and we can call those aspects being, doing, and having.

Being is the basic experience of being alive and conscious. It is the experience we have when we're fully focused in the present moment, the experience of being totally complete and at rest within ourselves.

Doing is movement and activity. It stems from the natural creative energy that flows through every living thing and is the source of our vitality.

Having is the state of being in relationship with other people and things in the universe. It is the ability to allow and accept things and people into our lives; to comfortably occupy the same space with them.

Being, doing, and having are like a triangle where each side supports the others.

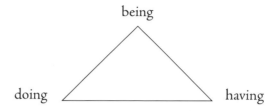

They are not in conflict with each other.
They all exist simultaneously.

Often people attempt to live their lives backward: They try to *have* more things, or more money, in order to *do* more of what they want, so that they will *be* happier.

The way it actually works is the reverse. You must first *be* who you really are, then *do* what you need to do, in order to *have* what you want.

The purpose of creative visualization is:

To connect us with our being.
To help us focus and facilitate our doing.
To deepen, expand, and align our having.

THREE NECESSARY ELEMENTS

There are three elements within you that determine how successfully creative visualization will work for you in any given situation:

1. Desire. You must have a true desire to have or create that which you have chosen to visualize. Ask yourself, "Do I truly, in my heart, desire this goal to be realized?"

2. Belief. The more you believe in your chosen goal and the possibility of attaining it, the more certain you will be to do so. Ask yourself, "Do I believe that this goal can exist?" and "Do I believe that it is possible for me to realize or attain it?"

3. Acceptance. You must be willing to *accept* and *have* that which you are seeking. Sometimes we pursue goals

without actually wanting to attain them. We are more comfortable with the process of pursuing. Ask yourself, "Am I really completely willing to *have* this?"

The sum total of these three elements is what I call your *intention*. When you have strong intention to create something — that is, you deeply desire it, you completely believe that you can do it, and you are totally willing to have it — it is very likely to manifest in your life in one way or another.

The clearer and stronger your intention, the more quickly and easily your creative visualization will work. In any given situation, ask yourself about the condition of your intention. If it is weak or uncertain, look more deeply to see what your doubts, fears, conflicts, or concerns may be. Sometimes your hesitations may be an indication of feelings and beliefs that need to be acknowledged and healed. In some cases, hesitation may be an indication that this is not a truly appropriate goal for you.

CONTACTING YOUR HIGHER SELF

One of the most important steps in making your creative visualization work effectively and successfully is to have the feeling of being connected with your inner spiritual source.

Your spiritual source is the supply of infinite love, wisdom, and energy in the universe. For you, "source" may mean God, Goddess, universal intelligence, the Great Spirit, the higher power, or your true essence. However we conceptualize it, it can be found here and now within each of us, in our inner beings.

You can think of contacting your source as connecting with your higher self, the wise being who dwells within you. Being in contact with your higher self is characterized by a deep sense of knowingness and certainty, of power, love, and wisdom. You know that you are creating your own experience of life and that you have the power to create the experiences most important and necessary for your own learning process.

We have all had experiences of being connected with our higher selves, although we may not have conceptualized it in that way. Feeling exceptionally high, clear, strong, "on top of the world," or "able to move mountains," are indications of being connected with your higher self; so is the experience of "falling in love"... when you feel wonderful about yourself and the world because your love for another human being is causing you to connect with your highest self.

When you first become consciously aware of the experience of your higher self, you will find that it seems to come and go rather sporadically. At one moment you may be feeling strong, clear, and creative, the next moment you may be thrown back into confusion and insecurity. This seems to be a natural part of the process. Once you are aware of your higher self, you can call on it whenever you need it, and gradually you will find that it is with you more and more of the time.

The connection between your personality and your higher self is a two-way channel, and it's important to develop the flow in both directions.

RECEPTIVE: When you quiet your personality during meditation, and come into a "being" space, you open the channel for higher wisdom and guidance to come to you through your intuitive mind. You can ask questions and wait for answers to come to you through words, mental images, or feeling impressions.

ACTIVE: When you are experiencing yourself as the cocreator of your life, you make choices about what you desire to create, and channel the infinite energy, power, and wisdom of your higher self into manifesting your choices through active visualization and affirmation.

When the channel is flowing freely in both directions, you are being guided by your higher wisdom, and based on that guidance, you are making choices and creating your world in the highest, most beautiful way.

Almost any form of meditation will eventually take you to an experience of your spiritual source, or your higher self. If you are not sure what this experience feels like, don't worry about it. Just continue to practice your relaxation, visualization, and affirmations. Eventually you will start experiencing certain moments during your meditations when there is a sort of "click" in your consciousness and you feel like things are really working; you may even experience a lot of energy flowing through you or a warm, radiant glow in your body. These are signs that you are beginning to channel the energy of your higher self.

Here's an exercise in creative visualization that will help you tune into the feeling. You might wish to do this exercise regularly at the beginning of your meditation periods:

51

Sit or lie in a comfortable position. Relax completely... let all tension drain out of your body and mind ... breathe deeply and slowly... relax more and more deeply.

Visualize a light within your heart — glowing radiant and warm. Feel it spreading and growing — shining out from you farther and farther until you are like a golden sun, radiating loving energy on everything and everyone around you.

Say to yourself silently and with conviction, "Divine light and divine love are flowing through me and radiating from me to everything around me."

Repeat this over and over to yourself until you have a strong sense of your own spiritual energy. If you wish, use any other affirmations of your own power, light, or creative ability, such as,

God is working through me now.
I am filled with creative energy.
The light within me is creating miracles
in my life here and now.

Or use whatever phrase has meaning and power for you.

GOING WITH THE FLOW

The only effective way to use creative visualization is in the spirit of the way of the Tao — "going with the flow." That means that you don't have to exert effort to get where you want to go; you simply keep clearly in mind where you would like to go, and then patiently and harmoniously follow the flow of the river of life until it takes you there. The river of life sometimes takes a winding course toward your goal. It may even seem temporarily to be going in a different direction entirely, yet in the long run it is a more effortless and harmonious way to get there than through struggling and striving.

Going with the flow means holding onto your goals lightly (even though they may seem very important) and being willing to change them if something more appropriate and satisfying comes along. It is that balance between keeping your destination clearly in mind and yet enjoying all the beautiful scenes you encounter along the way, and even being willing to change your destination if life starts taking you in a different direction. In short, it means being firm, yet flexible.

If you have a lot of heavy emotions riding on whether you attain your goal (that is, if you will be very upset if you don't get what you want), you will tend to work against yourself. In your fear of *not* getting what you want, you may actually be energizing the idea of not getting it as much or more than you are energizing the goal itself.

If you do find yourself very emotionally attached to a goal, it may be most effective and appropriate to work first on your feelings about the matter. You may have to take a good look at what you fear about *not* achieving the goal, and do affirmations to help you feel more confident and secure, or to help you face your fears.

For example:

The universe is unfolding perfectly.

I don't have to hang on.

I can relax and let go.

I can go with the flow.

I trust my own process.

I always have everything I need.

I have all the love I need within my own heart.

I am a lovable and loving person.

I am whole in myself.

Divine love is guiding me and I am always taken care of.

The universe always provides.

You may find some of the clearing processes I give later helpful. And I refer you to my Recommended Resources section for books that may offer help and insight.

Of course it's perfectly okay to creatively visualize something to which you have a lot of emotional attachment — and it will sometimes work quite well. But if it doesn't, realize that you may be attempting to visualize something out of fear of what may happen if you *don't* get it. In this case, it's important to relax and accept your feelings, accept the idea that you may not immediately realize your goal, look more deeply into your fears, and understand that resolving the conflict is probably an important area of growth for you and a wonderful opportunity to get to know yourself on a deeper level.

At any time while doing creative visualization, if you get a feeling that you are trying to *force* or *push* something that doesn't want to happen, back off a little and ask your higher self whether or not this is really the best thing for you, or whether or not you truly desire it. You may not yet be truly ready for it, or the universe may be trying to show you something better that you haven't even considered.

A man recently told me this story: A few years ago he was trying to make it as a stand-up comedian. He bought this book, and tried to visualize himself as a successful comedian. Try as he might, he simply couldn't get a clear picture or feeling of this happening. He took this as a message to re-examine his goals. After much soul-searching, he returned to school and became a minister and psychotherapist, which he loves. Now he is also a talk show host on a popular national television show that focuses on metaphysical and paranormal phenomena. This unusual combination of careers suits him perfectly! In this case, not being able to visualize what he thought he wanted helped him find a whole new direction in his life. This story is also a good example of how we may not know exactly what we want; we have to keep allowing the process to unfold.

PROSPERITY

A very important part of the whole creative visualization process is developing a sense of prosperity. This means having the understanding, or consciously taking the point of view, that the universe is abundant, that life is actually *trying* to bring us what our hearts and souls truly desire — spiritually, mentally, emotionally, as well as physically. Almost everything you *truly* need or want is here for the asking; you only need to *believe* that it is so, truly desire it, and be willing to *accept* it.

One of the most common causes of failure when seeking what you want is "scarcity programming." This is an attitude or set of beliefs about life that goes something like this:

There isn't enough to go around....

Life is suffering....

It is immoral or selfish to have enough when others don't....

Life is hard, difficult, a vale of tears....

You must work hard and sacrifice for everything you gain. . . .

It's more noble and spiritual to be poor. . . .

These are all false beliefs. They are based on a lack of understanding of how the universe works, or a misunderstanding of some important spiritual principles. These beliefs are not of service to you or anyone else; they simply limit *all of us* from realizing our natural state of prosperity and plenty on all levels.

At the present time there is a reality in this world of starvation and poverty for many people, *but we do not need to keep creating and perpetuating that reality.* The fact is that there is more than enough to go around for every being on earth, if we are willing to open our minds to that possibility, and change our ways of using and distributing the world's resources. The universe is a place of great abundance and we are all meant to be naturally prosperous, both in material and spiritual wealth, *in a way that is balanced and harmonious with one another and with the earth that nourishes us.*

In modern times, humankind has lost touch with its natural state of prosperity. Together, we are creating a world vastly out of balance, in which a relative few have far more than they need and are using up our natural resources at an alarming rate, while the majority suffer from serious lack. We are all responsible for creating this reality, and we can change it by changing both our way of thinking and our way of living. We need to reclaim our ability to appreciate and enjoy the simple pleasures in life. Many of us in the industrialized world need to cultivate a simpler, more natural lifestyle. We need to realize that after our basic needs are met, the experience of abundance has more to do with expressing our creative gifts in satisfying ways, and learning to give and receive in a balanced way, than it does with extravagant consumerism.

The truth about this earth is that it is an infinitely good, beautiful, nourishing place to be. The only "evil" comes from a lack of understanding of this truth. Evil (ignorance) is like a shadow — it has no real substance of its own; it is simply a lack of light. You cannot cause a shadow to disappear by trying to fight it, by stamping on it, by railing against it, or by any other form of emotional or physical resistance. In order to cause a shadow to disappear, you must shine light on it.

Take a look at your belief system and see if you are holding yourself back by not believing sufficiently in the possibility of prosperity. Can you actually realistically imagine yourself as a successful, satisfied, fulfilled person? Can you really open your eyes to the goodness and beauty and abundance that are all around you? Can you imagine this world transformed into a prosperous and supportive environment in which *everyone* can flourish?

You will experience difficulty in creating what you want in your personal life unless you view the world as a good place to be and a place that works for everyone.

This is because human nature is basically loving, and so most of us will not allow ourselves to have what we want as long as we believe that we might be depriving others in order to do so.

We have to understand in a deep way that having what we truly want in life contributes to the general state of human happiness and supports others in creating more happiness for themselves.

To create prosperity, we need to visualize ourselves living as we desire to live, doing what we love, feeling satisfied with what we attain, in a context of other people doing the same.

In a spirit of fun, try this exercise to stimulate your imagination and expand your ability to visualize true prosperity:

59

ABUNDANCE MEDITATION

Relax completely in a comfortable position.

Picture yourself in any lovely natural environment — perhaps by a green, open meadow with a lovely brook, or on white sand by the ocean. Take some time to imagine all the beautiful details, and see yourself fully enjoying and appreciating your surroundings. Now begin to walk, and soon find yourself in some totally different surrounding environment, perhaps exploring a waving field of golden grain, or swimming in a lake. Continue to wander and explore — finding more and more exquisitely beautiful environments of great variety — mountains, forests, deserts, whatever suits your fantasy. Take a little time to appreciate each one.

Now imagine returning home to a simple but comfortable and lovely environment, whatever would most suit you. Imagine having loving family, friends, and community around you. Visualize yourself doing work that you love, and expressing yourself creatively in ways that feel just right for you. You are being amply rewarded for your efforts, in internal satisfaction, appreciation from others, and financial return. Imagine yourself feeling fulfilled and thoroughly enjoying your life. Step back, and see if you can imagine a world full of people living simply yet abundantly, in harmony with one another and the earth.

AFFIRMATIONS

I find prosperity in simplicity.

This is an abundant universe and there is plenty for all of us.

God is the unfailing, unlimited source of all my supply.

*Abundance is my true state of being. I am now ready
to accept it fully and joyously.*

*I deserve to be prosperous and happy. I am now
prosperous and happy!*

The more I prosper, the more I have to share with everyone else.

*I'm ready now to accept all the joy and prosperity life
has to offer me.*

*The world is now becoming an abundant place
for everyone.*

Financial success is coming to me easily and effortlessly.

I am now enjoying financial prosperity!

Life is meant to be fun and I'm now willing to enjoy it!

I am rich in consciousness and manifestation.

*I now have plenty of money for my own personal needs
and the needs of my family.*

I now have a satisfying income of $ _____ per month.

I feel deeply satisfied with my financial situation.

I feel rich, well, and happy.

ACCEPTING YOUR GOOD

In order to use creative visualization to create what you want in life, you must be willing and able to *accept* the best that life has to offer you — your "good."

Strange as it may seem, many of us have difficulty accepting the possibility of having what we want in life. This usually stems from some basic feelings of unworthiness which we took on at a very early age. The basic belief goes something like this: "I'm really not a very good (lovable, worthwhile) person, so I don't deserve to have what I want."

This belief is usually mixed with other, sometimes contradictory, feelings that you really are perfectly good and deserving. But if you find that you have any difficulty imagining yourself in the most wonderful possible circumstances, or that you have thoughts like, "I could never have that," or "That couldn't possibly happen to me," it might be a good idea to take a look at your self-image.

Your self-image is the way you see yourself, how you feel about yourself. It is often complex and multifaceted. To get in touch with different aspects of your self-image, begin to ask yourself, "How do I feel about myself right now?" at various times throughout the day, and in various different situations. Just begin to notice what kinds of ideas or images you hold in mind about yourself at different times.*

One very interesting and revealing action to take is to get in touch with your *physical* images of yourself by asking, "How do I look to myself right now?" If you find yourself feeling awkward, ugly, fat, skinny, too big, too small, or whatever, it may be a clue to the fact that you aren't loving yourself enough to give yourself what you truly deserve — the best. It is often astounding to me to discover how many perfectly beautiful, attractive people frequently think of themselves as ugly, unworthy, undeserving.

Affirmations and creative visualization are wonderful ways of creating a more positive and loving self-image. Once you get in touch with the ways in which you are not loving yourself, begin to take every opportunity to make positive, appreciative, loving statements to yourself. Notice when you are being mentally harsh or critical with yourself, and consciously begin being kinder and more appreciative. You will find this immediately helps you to be more loving toward others, as well.

Think of specific qualities that you do appreciate about yourself. In the same way that you can love a good friend while clearly seeing his or her faults and shortcomings, you can love yourself for all that you truly are, while still being aware that there are ways you

---

* I highly recommend the book *Embracing Your Inner Critic* and/or the CD *Meet Your Inner Critic* by Dr. Hal Stone and Dr. Sidra Stone, listed in the Recommended Resources section of this book.

need to grow and develop. It feels very good to do this for yourself, and it can really work wonders in your life.

Begin to tell yourself:

I am lovable.

I am kind and loving, and I have a great deal to share with others.

I am talented, intelligent, and creative.

I am attractive.

I deserve the very best in life.

I have a lot to offer and everyone recognizes it.

I love the world and the world loves me.

I am willing to be happy and successful.

Or use whatever words seem appropriate and helpful to you.

It is often very effective to do this type of affirmation in the second person, using your own name. For example:

Susan, you are a brilliant and interesting person.
I like you very much.

John, you are so warm and loving.
People really appreciate that about you.

This way of talking directly to yourself is especially effective because much of our negative self-image comes from being convinced in various ways by other people that we are bad, stupid, or inadequate in some way.

Try to picture yourself as clearly as you can, and think of giving love to yourself, the same way you would to anyone else you care for.

65

You might think of it as the parent in you giving love and appreciation to the child in you.

Tell yourself:

I love you. You are a very beautiful person.
I appreciate your sensitivity and honesty.

Creative visualization is a great way to work on any physical problems you may feel you have. For example, if you feel you are overweight, you could use two approaches simultaneously:

1.   Through affirmations and loving energy, start learning to love and appreciate yourself more as you already are.

2.   Through creative visualization and affirmations, start imagining yourself as you want to be — fit, healthy, and happy. These techniques can be extremely effective in making real changes.*

These same two techniques hold true for working on any aspect of yourself with which you are not satisfied.

Remember, you are a new person at every new moment. Every day is a new day, and each one is an opportunity to realize the wonderful, loving, and lovable person you truly are....

In addition to improving your self-image, it is valuable to repeat affirmations about opening up to and accepting the goodness of the universe.

---

* Keep in mind that weight problems and many other physical issues often have deep emotional roots as well, and it may be important to reach out for help from a therapist or support group that specializes in these issues.

For example:

I am open to receiving the blessings
of this abundant universe.

Everything good is coming to me easily and effortlessly.
(Any word you want can be substituted
for "everything good," such as love,
prosperity, creativity, or a loving relationship.)

I accept my good, which is flowing to me here and now.

I deserve the best and the best is coming to me now.

The more I receive, the more I have to give.

Here is a meditation you can do to improve your self-esteem and increase your capacity to handle the love and energy that the universe is ready and eager to send in your direction:

SELF-APPRECIATION MEDITATION

Imagine yourself in some everyday situation, and picture someone (maybe someone you know, or a stranger) looking at you with great love and admiration and telling you something they really like about you. Now picture a few more people coming up and agreeing that you are a very wonderful person. (If this embarrasses you, stick with it.) Imagine more and more people arriving and gazing at you with tremendous love and respect in their eyes. Picture yourself in a parade or on a stage, with throngs of cheering, applauding people, all loving and appreciating you. Hear their applause ringing in your ears. Stand up and take a bow, and thank them for their support and appreciation.

Here are some affirmations for self-appreciation:

I love and accept myself completely as I am.

*I don't have to try to please anyone else. I like myself
and that's what counts.*

*I am highly pleasing to myself in the presence of
other people.*

I express myself freely, fully, and easily.

I am a powerful, loving, and creative being.

OUTFLOWING

Another key principle is that of giving, or "outflowing." The universe is made of pure energy, the nature of which is to move and flow. The nature of life is constant change, constant flux. When we understand this, we tune into its rhythm and we are able to give and receive freely, knowing that we never really lose anything, but constantly gain.

Once we begin to learn to *accept* the goodness of the universe, we naturally want to *share* it as well, realizing that as we give out of our energy, we make space for more to flow into us.

When, through insecurity (fear) and a feeling that there "isn't enough," we try to hold onto or cling to what we have, we begin to cut off this wonderful flow of energy. In the process of hanging onto what we have, we fail to keep the energy moving and we don't make space for new energy to come to us.

Energy takes many forms, such as love, affection, appreciation and recognition, material possessions, money, and friendship. The principles apply equally to all these forms.

If you look around you at those who are most unhappy, you'll often find that they are people who have a "starved" feeling in some way, and are therefore taking a very grasping posture toward life. They feel that life in general and other people in particular are not giving them what they need. It is as if they have a stranglehold on life, trying desperately to wring out the love and satisfaction they crave, yet actually choking off the supply. And many of us have a little of this tendency.

When we find that place within ourselves that is giving, we begin to reverse the flow. True giving happens not from a space of sacrifice, or self-righteousness, or an idea of spirituality, but for the pure *pleasure* of it — because it's fun. It can only come from a full, loving place.

We each have an infinite supply of love and happiness within us. We have been accustomed to thinking that we have to get something from outside of us in order to be happy, but in truth it works the other way: We must learn to contact our inner source of happiness and satisfaction, and flow it outward to share with others — *not because it is virtuous to do so, but because it feels really good!* Once we tune into it we just naturally want to share it because that is the essential nature of love, and we are all loving beings.

As we outflow our loving energy, we make room for more to flow into us. We soon discover that this process feels so good in itself we just want to do it more and more. And the more you share of yourself from this space, the more you seem to get from the world, because of the outflow-inflow principle. (Nature abhors a vacuum, so as you outflow you create space into which something must flow.) Giving becomes its own reward.

When we fully understand and live this principle, we have manifested our innately loving nature.

Remember, however, that giving from a healthy place means

being able to say "no" when *giving doesn't feel right, that you can't continue to give unless you are equally open to receiving . . . and that "giving" also means giving to yourself.*

When it comes to outflowing, practice makes perfect. You must consciously practice it in order to get the experience of how good it feels. Here are some exercises in outflowing you can try if you need some expansion in this area:

1. Make a point to express more appreciation to others in as many ways as you can think of. Sit down right now and make a list of people to whom you would like to outflow love and appreciation, and think of a way you can do so to each one within the next week. Outflow can take the form of words, touching, a gift, a phone call or letter, money, or any sharing of your talents that makes another person feel good. Choose something that makes you feel especially good too, even if it's a little more difficult for you.

    Practice speaking more words of thanks, appreciation, and admiration to people when you feel like it. "It was kind of you to help me." "I want you to know that I appreciate that." "Your eyes were shining and beautiful as you said that, and it made me feel good to see you." (It's okay to say these things even if you feel a little embarrassed!)

2. Go through your personal possessions and find items you don't really want or don't use very often, and give them to others who will appreciate them more.

3. If you're a person who tries to spend as little money as possible and always hunts for a bargain, try spending a

little money each day unnecessarily. Buy the product that costs a few cents more instead of less, treat yourself to a little something extra, pay for a friend's coffee, or donate money to a good cause. Even a small action of this sort is a visible demonstration to yourself that you have faith in the abundance that you have been affirming. Actions speak as loud as words in this case.

4. Tithe your income. Tithing is the practice of giving a percentage of your income to a church, spiritual organization, or any group or person that you feel is making a worthwhile contribution in the world. It is a way of supporting that energy, and at the same time acknowledging that all you receive comes from the universe (or God); therefore, you give a token back to the universal source. It doesn't matter what the percentage is. Even tithing just 1 percent of your income will give you a continuous experience of outflowing.

5. Be creative. Think of other ways to outflow your energy into the universe for the good of yourself and others.

HEALING

Creative visualization is one of the most important tools we have for creating and maintaining good health.

One of the basic principles of holistic health is that we cannot separate our physical health from our emotional, mental, and spiritual states of being. All levels are interconnected and often a state of "dis-ease" in the body is a reflection of conflict, tension, anxiety, or disharmony on other levels of being as well. So when we have a physical disorder, it is inevitably a message for us to look deeply into our emotional and intuitive feelings, our thoughts and attitudes, to see what we can do to restore natural harmony and balance to our beings. We must tune in and "listen" to the inner process.

Creative visualization is one way in which we communicate from our minds to our bodies. It is the process of forming images and thoughts in our minds, consciously or unconsciously, and then transmitting them to our bodies as signals or commands.

Conscious creative visualization is the process of creating

positive thoughts and images to communicate with our bodies, in place of negative, constrictive, literally "sickening" ones.

HEALING OURSELVES

Sometimes, we get sick because we believe on an inner level that illness is an appropriate or inevitable response to some situation or circumstance, because it in some way seems to solve a problem for us, or gets us something that we need, or because it is a solution to some unresolved and unbearable inner conflict.

Some examples of this are: the person who becomes ill because he has been exposed to a communicable disease (and thus believes his illness is inevitable or highly likely); the person who dies of the same disease a parent or other member of her family had (because she has unconsciously programmed herself to follow the same pattern); the person who gets sick or has an accident in order to get out of work (either there's something he can't confront at work, or he won't allow himself the necessary relaxation and quiet time unless he is sick); the person who gets sick in order to get love and attention (this was how she was able to get her parents' love as a child); the person who represses his feelings all his life and eventually dies of cancer (he cannot resolve the conflict between the pressure of his stored-up emotions and the belief that it's not okay for him to express those emotions).

I do not mean to imply by these examples that I believe all illness is a simple problem with a pat explanation. As with all our problems, there are many complex factors. I do intend to illustrate the fact that illness is a result of emotional, mental, and spiritual factors as well as physical ones, and that illness may be an attempt to find a solution to a problem we are having inside ourselves or in our lives. If we are willing to recognize and look deeply into our feelings and beliefs, we can often find healing on all levels.

The natural outgrowth of this point of view is a more constructive attitude about illness. Rather than thinking of ourselves as "victims," or of illness as an inevitable disaster or unavoidable misfortune, we think of it as a powerful and useful message. If we are suffering physically in some way, it is a message that there is something to be looked at within our consciousness, something to be recognized, acknowledged, and healed.

Often the message of illness is to be quieter and spend some time just being in contact with our inner selves. Illness often forces us to relax, let go of all our busyness and "efforting," and drop into a deep, quiet level of consciousness where we can receive the nourishing energy that we need.

The fundamental healing always comes from within, even though we may also require external treatment. When we allow ourselves quietness and inner contact regularly, we may no longer need to get sick in order for our inner selves to get our attention.

Illness and "accidents" are often messages that some inner problem needs to be resolved. Perhaps there are repressed feelings that need to be experienced, or there is some way we need to take better care of ourselves. Get as quiet as you can, listen for your inner voice, and ask what the message is, or what it is that you need to understand in this situation. You may be able to accomplish this alone, or in some cases you may need a counselor, therapist, friend, or healer to assist and support you.

It's important to understand that you are not "guilty" of creating, or "to blame" for, any illness or physical problem you may have. Your sickness is not an indication that you are an unconscious person. Instead, think of it as an important part of your evolutionary journey, a gift that can help you learn and grow.*

Creative visualization can be an effective tool for healing because it goes straight to one source of the problem — your own mental concepts and images. Begin to picture yourself and affirm to yourself that you are in good health; see your problem as completely healed and cured. There are many different approaches that can be taken on many different levels; you need to find the particular type of affirmations and images that work best for you. I've given some suggestions in Part Three of this book, and you can find others in the Recommended Resources section.

Of course, "preventative medicine" is always the best. . . . If you have no health problems, so much the better; simply affirm and visualize that you will always remain healthy and vital; that way you may never have to worry about healing yourself. If you already have health problems, it will be comforting to know that many "miraculous" cures are being accomplished every day — even for very serious illnesses such as cancer, arthritis, and heart disease — through the use of various forms of creative visualization.

Over the years since *Creative Visualization* was first published, hundreds of people have told me stories of how the ideas and techniques in the book have helped them heal themselves of serious illnesses and injuries. For example, a woman who came to one of my workshops had been in a serious automobile accident, was in a coma for a period of time, and was told by her doctors that she would require years of recuperation before she could hope to function

---

* For a more in-depth exploration, please read my book *The Four Levels of Healing*.

normally, if ever. Using creative visualization along with physical therapy, she fully recovered and returned to work within three months.

A man wrote to me with this story: He had been diagnosed with an inoperable brain tumor. The shock of this diagnosis caused him to look deeply at his life and recognize where he was feeling stuck and frustrated. He used the techniques from this book (along with his regular medical care) to help him resolve some of his life issues. The tumor eventually disappeared and several years later had not returned.

Many people have told me that after they were diagnosed with terminal cancer, they began using creative visualization techniques. Years later, they are alive and healthy. My own mother dissolved her gallstones without surgery, using visualization. When the doctor looked at the "before" X-rays (with gallstones) and the X-rays taken after she had been using visualization for a period of time (no gallstones), he simply couldn't believe it.

Of course, these healings could have been due to many factors. However, the number of stories and my own experience leads me to believe that visualization can be an effective tool.

In some cases, creative visualization may be a completely effective therapy in itself. In other cases, it is necessary to use other forms of treatment as well. As long as you have an inner confidence in some form of therapy, then by all means use it! It is likely to work if you desire it to and believe it will. Do not postpone appropriate medical treatment when it is called for! But whatever type of treatment is used — from conventional medicine or surgery to more holistic therapies such as acupuncture, yoga, massage, diet, and so on — creative visualization is always a helpful supplement, one that you can use in conjunction with the treatment of your choice. Conscious use of creative visualization can speed and smooth the normal healing process amazingly.

Keep in mind that not all ailments are meant to be "healed" in the sense of getting well or getting over them. Some may serve an important purpose in our lives, or in our soul's journey, and may stay with us for a long time, or for life. In this case, we may need to use visualization and affirmation to help us accept our limitations, and live the happiest or most rewarding lives possible.

Remember also that every one of us at some time must make the transition from physical life into another realm. Most people at this time make this transition through the vehicle of an illness. If someone has made the decision on a deep (usually unconscious) level that it is time to leave this life, it may be inappropriate or ineffective for them to try to "heal themselves" or for their loved ones to try to heal them. If attempts to heal seem ineffective, there may come a time to focus on visualizing a peaceful, satisfying completion of life and embracing of death.

HEALING OTHERS

The same principles that work in healing ourselves also work in healing others.

This is so because of the oneness nature of the universal mind. There is a part of our consciousness that is directly linked with that part in everyone else's consciousness. Since that part is also our link with divine omnipotence and omniscience, we *all* have incredible healing power that we can tap into at will.

It is an amazing thing, but simply changing your own concepts about another person and consciously holding and projecting an image of health and well-being can *instantly cure* someone in many cases, and speed and smooth their healing in many other cases. It is not even necessary for them to know anything about what you are doing; in fact, in some cases it may be better if the person who is ill doesn't consciously know.

I was brought up with a very scientific and rational background and education, and the ability to heal other people at a distance has been one of the hardest things for me to understand and accept. Yet I have seen it and experienced it too often to doubt it any longer. And there are interesting scientific studies that confirm the healing power of prayer and visualization.*

In my experience, I've found that the best way to work on healing is to picture myself as a clear channel for healing energy, and envision the spiritual energy of the universe flowing through me to the person who needs it. I think of my higher self sending energy to the other person's higher self to support them in whatever they need to do to heal themselves, keeping in mind that it's okay if the person chooses *not* to get well. At the same time, I picture the person as he or she truly is ... a divine being, a beautiful and perfect expression of God ... naturally healthy and happy.

79

In Part Three, I describe the healing methods that I have found work best for me. I encourage you to try them, and to discover your own.

---

* See *Healing Words: The Power of Prayer and the Practice of Medicine,* by Larry Dossey, MD. See the Recommended Resources section of this book.

Meditations and Affirmations

Thou shalt decree a thing,
and it shall be established unto thee:
and the light shall shine upon thy ways.

— Job 22:28

GROUNDING YOURSELF
AND RUNNING ENERGY

This is a very simple visualization technique, and one which is good to do at the beginning of any meditation. The purpose of it is to get your energy flowing, dissolve any blocks, and keep you firmly connected to the physical plane so that you don't "space out" during meditation.

Sit comfortably with your back straight, either in a chair or cross-legged on a pillow on the floor. Close your eyes, breathe slowly and deeply, counting down from ten to one until you feel deeply relaxed.

Imagine that there is a long cord attached to the base of your spine, extending down through the floor and way down into the earth. If you wish, you can imagine that this is like the root of a tree, growing deep into the ground. This is called a "grounding cord."

Now imagine that the energy of the earth is flowing up

through this cord (and up through the soles of your feet, if you are sitting in a chair) and flowing up through all parts of your body, and out through the top of your head. Picture this until you really feel the flow well established. Now imagine that the energy of the cosmos is flowing in through the top of your head, through your body, and down through your grounding cord and your feet into the earth. Feel both these flows going in different directions, and mixing harmoniously in your body.

This meditation keeps you balanced between the cosmic energy of vision, fantasy, and imagination and the stable, earthy energy of the physical plane . . . a balance that will increase your sense of well-being and your power of manifestation.

OPENING THE ENERGY CENTERS

This is a meditation for healing and purifying your body, and for getting your energy flowing. It is an excellent exercise to do in the morning when you first wake up, or at the beginning of any meditation period, or anytime you want to be relaxed and refreshed.

Lie down on your back with arms at your sides or with hands clasped on your stomach. Close your eyes, relax, and breathe gently, deeply, and slowly.

Imagine that there is a glowing sphere of golden light surrounding the top of your head. Breathe deeply and slowly in and out five times while you keep your attention on the sphere of light, feeling it radiate from the top of your head.

Now allow your attention to move down to your throat. Again imagine a golden sphere of light emanating from your throat area. Breathe slowly in and out five times with your attention on this light.

Allow your attention to move down to the center of your chest. Once again imagine the golden light, radiating from the center of your chest. Again take five deep breaths, as you feel the energy expanding more and more.

Next put your attention on your solar plexus or the area of your navel; visualize the sphere of golden light all around your midsection. Breathe into it slowly, five times.

Now visualize the light glowing in and around your pelvic area. Again take five deep breaths, feeling the light energy radiating and expanding.

Finally, visualize the glowing sphere of light around your feet, and breathe into it five more times.

Now imagine all six of the spheres of light glowing at once so that your body is like a strand of jewels, radiating energy.

Breathe deeply and, as you exhale, imagine energy flowing down along the outside of one side of your body from the top of your head to your feet. As you inhale, imagine it flowing up along the other side of your body to the top of your head. Circulate it around your body this way three times.

Then visualize the flow of energy going from the top of your head down along the front of your body to your feet as you slowly exhale. As you inhale, feel it flow up along the back of your body to the top of your head. Circulate the flow in this direction three times.

Now imagine that the energy is gathering at your feet, and let it flow slowly up through the center of your body from your feet to your head, radiating from the top of your head like a fountain of light, then flowing back down the outside of your body to your feet. Repeat this several times, or as long as you wish.

When you finish this meditation you will be deeply relaxed, yet energized and exhilarated.

87

CREATING YOUR SANCTUARY

One of the first things you should do when you start using creative visualization is to create a sanctuary within yourself where you can go anytime you want to. Your sanctuary is your ideal place of relaxation, tranquillity, and safety, and you can create it exactly as you want it.

> Close your eyes and relax in a comfortable position. Imagine yourself in some beautiful natural environment. It can be any place that appeals to you . . . in a meadow, on a mountaintop, in the forest, beside the sea. It could even be under the ocean, or on another planet. Wherever it is, it should feel comfortable, pleasant, and peaceful to you. Explore your environment, noticing the visual details, the sounds and smells, any particular feelings or impressions you get about it.
>
> Now do anything you would like to do to make the place more homelike and comfortable. You might want to

build some type of house or shelter there, perhaps just surround the whole area with a golden light of protection and safety, create and arrange things there for your convenience and enjoyment, or do a ritual to establish it as your special place.

From now on this is your own personal inner sanctuary, to which you can return anytime just by closing your eyes and desiring to be there. You will always find it healing and relaxing to be there. It is also a place of special power for you, and you may wish to go there every time you do creative visualization.

You may find that your sanctuary spontaneously changes from time to time, or that you want to make changes and additions to it. You can be very creative in your sanctuary and have a lot of fun there...just remember to retain the primary qualities of peacefulness, tranquillity, and a feeling of absolute safety.

MEETING YOUR GUIDE

All of us have tremendous wisdom and knowledge right within us. It is available to us through the intuitive mind, which is our connection with the Universal Intelligence. However, we often find it difficult to connect with our higher wisdom. One of the best ways to do so is by meeting and getting to know our inner guide.

The inner guide is known by many different names, such as your counselor, spirit guide, imaginary friend, or master. It is a wise part of yourself, which can come to you in many different forms, but usually comes in the form of a person or being whom you can talk to and relate to as a wise and loving friend.

Here is an exercise to help you meet your spirit guide. If you wish, you can have a friend read this to you while you do the meditation. Otherwise, read through it first, close your eyes, and do it.

Close your eyes and relax deeply. Go to your inner sanctuary and spend a few minutes there, relaxing, getting oriented.

Now imagine that within your sanctuary you are standing on a path that stretches off into the distance. You start to walk up the path, and as you do, you see in the distance a form coming toward you, radiating a clear, bright light.

As this form approaches, you begin to see whether the form is a man or a woman — or perhaps an animal. If it's a person, how old are they? And how are they dressed? The closer the form gets, the more details you can see of the face and appearance.

Greet this being, and ask what his or her name is. Take whatever name comes to you first, and don't worry about it.

Now show your guide around your sanctuary and explore it together. Your guide may point out some things that you've never seen there before, or you may enjoy just being in each other's presence.

Ask your guide if there is anything he or she would like to say to you, or any advice he or she would like to give you at the moment. If you wish, you can ask some specific questions. You may get immediate answers but, if not, don't be discouraged — the answers will come to you in some form later.

When the experience of being together feels complete for now, thank your guide and express your appreciation, and ask him or her to come to meet you in your sanctuary again.

Open your eyes and return to the outside world.

People have many different types of experiences when meeting their guides, so it is difficult to generalize. Basically if you feel good about your experience, then it's fine. If not, be creative and do whatever you need to do to change it.

Don't worry if you did not perceive your guide clearly and

precisely. Sometimes they remain in the form of a glow of light, or a blurry, indistinct figure. The important thing is that you sense your guide's power, presence, and love.

If your guide should come to you in the form of someone you know, that is fine, *unless* you don't feel particularly good about it. In that case, repeat the exercise and request that your guide come to you in a form that is easy and pleasant for you to relate to.

If the figure you encounter in your meditation seems judgmental, harsh, or unloving, you may have contacted your inner critic or some other energy. Politely thank them for their input, let them go, and ask for a loving, supportive, encouraging guide to come.

Don't be surprised if your guide seems eccentric or unusual in some way... the form in which they show themselves to us springs from our own creative mind, which is limitless. For example, your guide may have a very unusual and surprising sense of humor, or an exotic name and a flair for the dramatic. Sometimes they don't communicate in words at all, but in a direct transmission of feeling impressions or intuitive knowledge.

Also, your guide *may* change form, and even name, from time to time. Or you may have the same one for years. You may have more than one guide at the same time.

Your guide is there for you to call on anytime you need or want extra clarity, wisdom, knowledge, support, creative inspiration, love, or companionship. Many people who have established relationships with their guides meet them every day in their meditation.

93

PINK BUBBLE TECHNIQUE

This meditation exercise is simple and wonderfully effective.

Sit or lie down comfortably, close your eyes, and breathe deeply, slowly, and naturally. Gradually relax deeper and deeper.

Imagine something that you would like to manifest. Imagine that it has already happened. Picture it as clearly as possible in your mind.

Now, in your mind's eye, surround your fantasy with a pink bubble; put your goal inside the bubble. Pink is the color associated with the heart, and if this color vibration surrounds whatever you visualize, it will bring to you only that which is in perfect affinity with your being.

The third step is to let go of the bubble and imagine it floating off into the universe, still containing your vision.

This symbolizes that you are emotionally "letting go" of it. Now it is free to float around in the universe, attracting and gathering energy for its manifestation.

There is nothing more you need to do.

HEALING MEDITATIONS

Here are some techniques that can be very effective for healing ourselves and others.

HEALING OURSELVES

This meditation can help us discover an underlying cause for an ailment and/or begin to release and heal it.

> Sit or lie down, breathe, and relax deeply. Starting with your toes, feet, legs, pelvis, and so on, put your attention on each part of your body in turn, and tell it to relax and let go of any tension. Feel all tension dissolving and draining away.
>
> If you wish to, do the meditation on opening the energy centers in order to get your energy really flowing.
>
> Now imagine golden, healing light energy all around your body... feel it... sense it... enjoy it.

If there is a particular part of your body that has been ill or is in pain, ask that part of you whether it has a message for you. Ask whether there is something you need to understand or to do, right at this moment or in your life in general. Remain quiet for a few minutes and notice if any words, images, or feelings come to you in response to these questions.

If you get an answer, do your best to understand and follow it. If you don't get an answer, just continue with the process. The answer may come to you later, perhaps in a different form than you expect.

Now send special loving, healing energy to that part of you, and any part of you that needs it, and see or feel it being healed. You may want to have your guide, or any master or healer, there to help you do the healing.

Picture the problem dissolving and flowing energy away, or whatever image works for you.

Now imagine yourself in natural, perfect health. Think of yourself in different situations feeling well, active, and healthy. Imagine nurturing and caring for yourself so you stay healthy.

AFFIRMATIONS

I am loving and healing myself on all levels —
spiritual, mental, emotional, and physical.

I honor and respect my body.

I listen to my body's messages.

I am learning to take good care of myself.

I love and accept my body completely.

I am good to my body, and my body is good to me.

I deserve to be healthy and feel good.

My body is balanced, in perfect harmony with the earth and the universe.

I give thanks for ever-increasing health, beauty, and vitality.

It's natural to feel good.

From now on, each time you do this meditation, picture yourself in perfect health, with golden healing light around you.

HEALING OTHERS

This meditation is to be done alone, not in the other person's presence, unless that person has requested this type of healing from you. You may or may not wish to tell the other person that you are doing healing meditations for them, depending on how well the person would accept that idea on a personality level.

Relax deeply and do whatever type of preparation you wish in order to enter a deep, quiet state of mind.

Think of yourself as a clear channel through which the healing energy of the universe is pouring. This energy does not come from you personally; it comes from a higher source, and you serve to focus and direct it.

Now picture or think of the person as clearly as you can. Ask him if there is anything in particular he would like you to do for him in your meditation. If so, do it to the best of your ability, if it feels right to you.

If you feel the impulse to work on healing a particular part of the person's body, or a particular problem, do so. Just see all problems dissolved, everything being healed and functioning perfectly.

Then picture him surrounded in golden, healing light ...looking radiantly healthy and happy. Speak to him directly (in your mind); remind him that he is being taken care of by a higher power, and that he can heal if he desires. Tell him that you support him in being totally healthy and happy, and that you will continue to send your loving support and energy.

When you feel complete, open your eyes and come back to the outer world feeling refreshed, renewed, healthy, and invigorated.

From now on, in your meditations, see the person as perfectly well. Don't give any more mental energy or power to the illness; just keep seeing him as completely healed.

You should not feel depleted from sending healing to another person, since it is not your own personal energy you are sending, but rather the universal life force flowing through you. If you do feel at all drained, you may be so emotionally involved that you are trying too hard. It might be helpful to imagine turning the healing of this person over to the higher power of the universe and affirming that whatever happens will be for his highest good. Remember, we can't always know what is the highest good for ourselves or another.

HEALING IN GROUPS

Healings are very powerful when done in groups.

If the person to be healed is present in the room, have her lie down in the center or sit in a chair (whichever is most comfortable), with everyone else seated in a circle around her.

Everyone should close their eyes, be quiet, and relax deeply, then begin to imagine sending healing energy to the person in the center. Remember that it is the healing energy of the universe that is being channeled through you. See the person surrounded in golden light, feeling well, and in perfect health.

If you wish, you can have everyone raise their hands with the palms facing out toward the person in the center, and feel the energy flowing out to her through your hands.

It can be especially powerful to have everyone chant "om" together for a few minutes while doing the healing, thus adding the healing vibration of sound to the process. (To chant "om" you sing a long, deep resonant note with the syllable a-a-aum-m, holding it as long as you can, repeating it over and over.) If this chanting is too difficult for people to do, it is definitely not necessary.

If the person is not present in the room, just inform everyone of her name and the city where she is, and then proceed as if she were there. The power of healing energy is not affected at all by distance, and I have seen as many miraculous cures accomplished for people in distant cities as for those present in the room.

HEALING MEDITATION FOR PAIN

Here is a meditation technique you can do with a person who is experiencing a headache or any other specific pain.

Have the person lie down, close his eyes, and relax deeply. Have him focus on his breath for a while, breathing deeply and slowly, yet naturally. Have him count down from ten to one slowly, feeling himself drift into a deeper, more relaxed state of being with each count.

When the person is very deeply relaxed, have him picture or imagine a bright color, any color (have him take the first color that comes to mind). Ask him to picture it as a sphere of bright light about six inches in diameter. Now ask him to picture it gradually growing bigger and bigger, until eventually it fills his whole field of mental vision. When he has experienced this, ask him to picture it shrinking, growing smaller and smaller, until it's back to its original size. Now have it grow smaller still, until it's only an inch or so in diameter, still shrinking, and finally disappearing completely.

Now go through the visualization exercise again, and this time have the person imagine that the color is his pain.

INVOCATIONS

To invoke means "to call in" or "to call upon." When used in meditation, invocation is a technique with which you can summon any type of energy or quality to come to you:

Close your eyes and relax deeply. Do some type of preparatory meditation such as grounding and running energy, or opening the energy centers, or simply going to your sanctuary, relaxing and breathing deeply for a while.

When you feel relaxed and energized, say to yourself silently, yet firmly and clearly, "*I now call forth the quality of love.*" Feel the energy of love coming to you, or coming out from some place inside of you, filling you up, and radiating out from you. Remain for a few minutes totally experiencing the feeling. Then, if you wish, direct it toward any particular goal through visualization and affirmation.

You can use the power of invocation to summon any quality or energy that you want or need . . .

strength

wisdom

serenity

compassion

softness

warmth

clarity

intelligence

creativity

healing power

Simply make a strong, clear statement to yourself that this quality is now coming to you.

Another wonderful way to use the power of invocation is to summon the spirit or essence of a particular person who has qualities that you desire. If you invoke one of the masters, such as Buddha, Christ, or Mary, you are calling forth the universal qualities which that person symbolizes, which also lie within each of us. For example, if you call for Christ to work in you and through you, you are summoning in a very powerful way your own qualities of love, compassion, forgiveness, and healing ability.

If there is any particular master or teacher or hero with whom you resonate, call upon him or her through invocation whenever you feel the need to manifest his or her special qualities within yourself.

This type of meditation works beautifully when there is a special skill or talent that you wish to cultivate. For example, if you are studying music or art, call upon any great master in these fields whom you especially admire; picture him or her supporting and helping you, and feel the person's creative energy and genius flowing through you. It is not necessary to incorporate any personal problems or weaknesses he or she may have had; you are summoning the person in his or her *highest aspect*. Many amazing results can be achieved through this meditation.

WAYS TO USE AFFIRMATIONS

There are so many ways that affirmations can be used powerfully and effectively to give you a more positive, creative outlook and to help you achieve specific goals.

Remember, it's important to feel *relaxed* as you affirm. Do not be addicted to getting the exact results that you want. Every process has its own timing and its own way of unfolding.

IN MEDITATION

Say affirmations to yourself silently while meditating or relaxing deeply, especially right before going to sleep or right after waking up.

SPOKEN

1. Say them to yourself, silently or aloud, throughout the day, whenever you think of it, especially while driving, doing housework, or during other routine tasks.

2. Say them to yourself aloud while looking at yourself in the mirror. This is especially good for affirmations to improve your self-esteem and self-love. Look yourself right in the eyes and affirm your beauty, lovableness, and worthiness. If you feel uncomfortable, stick with it until you push through those barriers and are able to fully experience looking at yourself and loving yourself. You may find that some emotion arises and is released through this process.

3. Record your affirmations on a tape recorder and play them to yourself around the house, while driving, and so on. Use your name, and try doing them in the first, second, and third persons. For example, "I, Shakti, am deeply relaxed and centered in myself." "Shakti, you are deeply relaxed and centered in yourself." "Shakti is deeply relaxed and centered in herself."

Or you can record a little speech, maybe three or four paragraphs long, describing your ideal visualization of yourself or a particular situation, as if it were already true. This also can be done in the first, second, and/or third person.

WRITTEN

1. Take a particular affirmation and write it out ten or twenty times in succession, *really thinking* about the words as you write them. Change the affirmation as you go along if you think of better ways to say it. This is one of the most powerful techniques I've ever found, and

one of the easiest to do. I've devoted a chapter to it in Part Four.

2. Write or type out affirmations and paste them up in various places around your house or at your job, as reminders. Good places are on the refrigerator, on your phone, on your mirror, on your desk, over your bed, or on your dining table.

WITH OTHERS

1. If you have a friend who wants to work on affirmations as well, you can do them very effectively with a partner. Sit facing each other, look into each other's eyes, and take turns saying affirmations to each other and accepting them.

    DAVID: *"Linda, you are a beautiful, loving, and creative person."*
    LINDA: *"Yes, I know!"* or *"Yes, I am!"*

    Repeat this ten or fifteen times the same way, then switch partners so that Linda says the affirmation to David and he agrees with it. Then try it in the first person:

    DAVID: *"I, David, am a beautiful, loving, and creative person."*
    LINDA: *"Yes, you certainly are."*

    Repeat several times.

    Be sure to say the affirmations sincerely and meaningfully, even if you feel a little silly at first. It's a wonderful opportunity to outflow love and support to another person, and to really support the other person in changing his or her negative concepts into positive ones.

It's practically guaranteed that after doing this process together, you will be experiencing a deep, loving space together....

2. In a more informal way, ask your friends to say affirmations to you frequently. For example, if you want to affirm that you are learning to express yourself more easily, you might ask a good friend to say to you often, "Jeannie, you are certainly speaking out and expressing yourself clearly these days!"

Make a game out of doing this for each other and you will find it helpful. We automatically tend to give a lot of power to what our friends say to us, for good or bad; our minds tend to accept what others tell us about ourselves. So getting strong positive feedback from friends in the form of affirmations really works.

3. Begin to include affirmations in your conversations — making strong positive statements about things and people (including yourself) that you want to see in a more positive way. It's amazing what dramatic changes can be made in your life by just beginning to consciously speak more positively in daily conversation.

A word of caution: Do not use this technique in such a way that you feel like you are contradicting your true feelings. Do not use it when you are feeling upset or strongly negative or it will feel like you are repressing yourself. Use it from a constructive space, to help change your unconscious negative speech patterns and underlying assumptions.

SINGING AND CHANTING

1. Make a point of learning songs that express deep feelings for you or that affirm the reality you would like to create for yourself; listen to them and sing them often.

2. Make up your own songs or simple chants using the affirmations you want to work with.

MORE AFFIRMATIONS

ACCEPTING OURSELVES

I accept myself completely here and now.

I love myself as I am.

I accept all my feelings as part of myself.

I'm beautiful and lovable however I'm feeling.

None of my feelings are negative. They are all important parts of who I am.

I am now willing to experience all my feelings.

It's good to express my feelings. I now give myself permission to express my feelings.

I love myself when I express my feelings.

FEELING GOOD

It's okay for me to have fun and enjoy myself, and I do!

I like to do things that make me feel good.

I am deeply relaxed and centered.

I now feel deep inner peace and serenity.

I'm glad I was born and I love being alive.

III

RELATIONSHIPS

My relationships are mirrors that show me myself.

I am now learning from all my relationships.

My relationships are helping me to heal and love myself.

I am strong, vulnerable, and loving in my relationships.

I deserve love and sexual pleasure.

I am now ready to accept a happy, fulfilling relationship.

I am now ready for my relationships to work.

I love myself and I naturally attract loving relationships into my life.

I am now attracting exactly the kind of relationship I want.

I am now divinely irresistible to my perfect mate.

All difficulties between me and _____ are now being healed.

The more I love myself, the more I love _____ .

I love _____ and _____ loves me.

OPENING CREATIVITY

I am now an open channel for creative energy.

*Creative ideas and inspiration are coming
to me every day.*

I am the creator of my life.

I am now creating my life exactly as I want it.

DIVINE LOVE AND GUIDANCE

*Divine love is doing its perfect work in this situation
now for the good of all concerned.*

Divine love and light are working through me now.

Divine love goes before me and prepares the way.

God is showing me the way now.

My inner wisdom is guiding me now.

*I am now being guided to the perfect solution to
this problem.*

*The light within me is creating miracles in my body, mind, and affairs,
here and now.*

PART FOUR

Special Techniques

If you would learn the secret of right relations,
look only for the divine in people and things,
and leave all the rest to God.

— J. Allen Boone, *Kinship with All Life*

A CREATIVE VISUALIZATION
NOTEBOOK

It's a very good idea to start a notebook that can serve as your creative visualization workbook.* In this part of the book, I give you a number of written exercises and processes that you might want to do and keep in your notebook. You may wish to write down affirmations that you hear or think of, so that you can refer to them when you need them. There are many other creative ways to use your notebook, such as recording your dreams, goals, and fantasies; keeping a journal of your progress with creative visualization; writing down inspiring thoughts and ideas, or quotes from books and songs that are meaningful to you; drawing pictures; or writing your own poems and songs that express your expanding awareness.

I have a notebook in which I regularly work on my goals,

---

* There is also a *Creative Visualization Workbook* available, published by Nataraj Publishing, a division of New World Library. See the Recommended Resources section of this book.

affirmations, ideal scenes, and treasure maps, and I have found it a very valuable tool in the transformation of my life.

Here are a few suggestions for starting your notebook:

1. Affirmations. Write down your favorite affirmations. You can list them all on one page, or you might want to make a separate page for each, with decorative borders and designs, so that each time you read through it you have a beautiful experience as you pause and meditate on each one.

2. Outflow list. Make a list of all the ways that you can outflow your energy to the world and to others around you, both generally and specifically. Include ways that you outflow money, time, love and affection, appreciation, physical energy, friendship, touching, and your special talents and abilities. Add to this list anytime you think of new things.

3. Success list. Make a list of everything you feel you are a success at, or have been a success at, or have done successfully at some time in your life. Include things in all areas of your life, not just your work. Write down everything that has meaning for you, even if it might not be meaningful to someone else. Keep adding to it as you think of more things, or accomplish new successes. The purpose of this list is to acknowledge yourself and your abilities, which gives you added energy for accomplishing more.

4. Appreciation list. Make a list of everything you can think of that you are especially thankful for, or that you

especially appreciate having in your life. Making and adding to this list can really open up your heart, and your awareness of the many riches we all have in our lives that we often take for granted. It increases your realization of prosperity and abundance on every level, and thus your ability to manifest.

5. Self-esteem list. Make a list of all the things you like about yourself, all your positive qualities. This is not an "ego trip" — the better you feel about yourself and the more you acknowledge your own wonderful qualities, the happier and more loving you will be, the more your creative energy will flow, and the greater the contribution you will make to the world.

6. Self-appreciation list. Write down all the ways you can think of to be good to yourself, nice things that you can do for yourself, simple indulgences that are just for your own pleasure and satisfaction. They can be small or large, but make some of them things you can easily do every day. And then do them! This increases your sense of well-being and satisfaction in life, which in turn helps you to come from a clearer space in creating your life.

7. Healing and assistance list. Write down the names of any people you know who need healing, or special support and assistance of any sort. Write down special affirmations for them. Every time you look through your notebook you will be giving them a special boost of your energy.

8. Fantasies and creative ideas. Jot down any ideas, plans, or dreams for the future, or any creative ideas that come

119

to you, even if they seem far-fetched, or you're sure you'll never follow through on them. This will help to loosen you up and stimulate your imagination and your natural creative ability.

You may find it difficult to take time out of your busy schedule to work in your notebook. Yet if you take a few minutes a day, or an hour or two every week or so, you will find that so much work is accomplished on the inner plane, it is often worth a hundred times the amount of time and energy you would have spent on the outer plane.

CLEARING

In learning to use creative visualization you may get in touch with blocks in yourself that hold you back from attaining your highest good.

A "block" is a place where energy is constricted — not moving, not flowing. Usually blocks are caused initially by repressed emotions of fear, sadness, guilt, self-criticism, and/or resentment (anger), which cause a person to tighten up and close down spiritually, mentally, emotionally, and even physically.

In dealing with a block on any level, what's needed is to get energy moving and flowing in that area. The keys to this are:

1. Mental and emotional acceptance of what you are feeling (on a physical level this manifests as relaxation and release).

2. Clear observation, which leads to an understanding of the root of the problem — which is often a limiting attitude or belief.

In dealing with an area of consciousness where we have a block, we need to first experience (as fully as possible) the emotion we have locked up in that area, in a loving, accepting way. In doing so, we get the blocked-up energy moving, and we have a chance to observe the underlying negative beliefs or attitudes that caused the problem to begin with. We can take a good, clear look at them and let them dissolve themselves.

Amazingly enough, it seems to be the process of pinpointing the constrictive belief and accepting the feelings you have around it that works magic; the difficulty almost inevitably dissolves and eventually disappears once you've understood and accepted yourself.

The trick is to simultaneously *love and accept yourself* compassionately for having this belief, and at the same time *see clearly that you are ready to let go of it* because it is limiting, destructive, self-defeating, and untrue.

Some common core beliefs that are most prevalent and troublesome are:

I'm not okay . . . there's something wrong with me . . .
I'm unworthy and undeserving.

I've done bad things (or a bad thing) in my life and I deserve to suffer
(be punished) for it.

People (including me) are basically bad — selfish, cruel,
stupid, untrustworthy, sinful, or foolish.

The world is an unsafe place.

Life is painful, suffering, hard work . . . it's not meant
to be fun or pleasurable.

Love is dangerous . . . I might get hurt.

Power is dangerous . . . I might hurt someone.

Money is the root of all evil. Money corrupts.

*The world doesn't work and never will. In fact, it's
getting worse all the time.*

*I don't have control over what happens to me . . . I'm
powerless to do anything about my life or the state
of the world.*

*There's not enough _____ (love, money, good things)
to go around, so:*

I have to struggle to get my share

or

It's hopeless, I'll never get enough

or

If I have a lot, someone else will have to do without.

As you read through these negative ideas, see whether any of them reflect an underlying assumption of your own belief system or emotional pattern.

Depressing though they may seem when you read through them all at once, the fact is that every one of us has bought into some of these (or other) negative viewpoints about reality, at least to some degree.

And it's no wonder that we have incorporated these ideas into our sense of reality — they are all extremely prevalent in our world at this time in our evolution. In fact, the world is currently being run according to these ideas, although fortunately this is changing.

The important thing to realize is that they are only beliefs; they have no objective truth. Although they may seem to be true at times when we look around us, that is only because so many human beings believe them and act accordingly.

The most powerful thing you can do (and it is very powerful) to change the world is to change your own beliefs about the nature of life, people, and reality, and begin to act accordingly.

This book will give you some tools to do so.

CLEARING EXERCISES

If you are having trouble realizing a goal, or sense resistance in yourself to its achievement, try this exercise:

1. Take a piece of paper and write at the top, "The reason I can't have what I want is . . . ," then immediately begin to write a list of any thoughts that come into your head to complete the sentence. Don't take too much time to write your answers, and don't take it too seriously. Just quickly write down about twenty or thirty things that come to you, even if they seem silly or stupid. A sample list might start like this:

  The reason I can't have what I want is . . .

I'm too lazy.

I don't have enough money.

It doesn't exist.

I've tried before and it never worked.

Mother said I couldn't.

I don't want to.

It's too hard.

I'm afraid to.

John wouldn't like it.

And so on. . . .

2. Try the same exercise, only this time specifically name the thing that you want. For example, "The reason I can't have a good job is . . ." and proceed as before.

   Now just sit quietly for a few minutes with your list and see whether any of the thoughts you've written down ring true for you . . . whether in some way or degree you believe them. Just get a sense of what kind of limitations you put on yourself and your world.

3. Now write a list of all the most negative attitudes you can think of about yourself, other people, relationships, the world, life.

   Again, sit quietly with your list and get in touch with which of these ideas may consciously or unconsciously hold emotional power over you.

   If at any point during any of these exercises you feel any emotion coming up, just stay with that and allow yourself to experience it as much as possible, with total acceptance. You may get a flash of an early experience, or something your parents or teachers used to tell you which programmed your view of the world in a certain way.

4. Whenever you feel complete with this process, especially if you've gotten in touch with one or more negative beliefs that you hold, simply tear up your lists and throw them away. This symbolizes that you are in the process of releasing them.

   Then sit quietly, relax, and do some affirmations to

125

replace your constricted, limiting beliefs with more opening, constructive, positive ones. A few possible clearing affirmations:

I am now releasing my past.

I am now dissolving all negative, limiting beliefs.

I now forgive and release everyone in my life.

I don't have to try to please others.
I am naturally lovable and likable no matter what I do!

I now let go of all accumulated guilt, fears, resentment, disappointments, and grudges. I am free and clear!

All of my negative self-images and attitudes are now dissolved.
I love and appreciate myself!

All barriers to my full expression and enjoyment of life are now dissolved.

The world is a beautiful place to be.

The universe always provides.

MORE CLEARING EXERCISES

1. This exercise is about forgiveness and release. Write down on a piece of paper the names of everyone in your life who you feel has ever mistreated you, harmed you, done you an injustice, or toward whom you feel or have felt resentment, hurt, or anger. Next to each person's name write down what he or she did to you, or what you resent the person for.

    Then close your eyes, relax, and one by one visualize

or imagine each person. Hold a little conversation with each one, and explain to him or her that in the past you have felt anger or hurt toward him or her, but now you are going to do your best to forgive the person for everything, and to dissolve and release all constricted energy between you. Give the person a blessing and say, "*I forgive you and release you. Go your own way and be happy.*"

When you have finished this process, write on your paper, "*I now forgive you and release you all*" and throw it away, as a symbol that you are letting go of these past experiences.

Many people find that this process of forgiveness and release is miraculous in relieving them immediately of their long-standing burdens of accumulated resentment and hostility. The wonderful thing is that the other people involved, even if you never see them again, will on a psychic level pick up your forgiveness, and it will help to clear up their lives as well.

It may be that the first time you do this process you will not have an experience of relief and release with certain people (especially a parent, spouse, or other very significant person in your life). If there is a strong emotional charge or a lot of deep feeling, it may be necessary to talk to a therapist or counselor, or find a safe place to fully express your anger and hurt. We mustn't try to force ourselves to forgive before we've really accepted and expressed our other feelings. After we do, forgiveness often comes naturally. Continue to do this process from time to time, and eventually it will be resolved for you. (Remember it is for your own benefit, health, and happiness that you are doing this.)

Many people experience miraculous healing of

physical problems after doing this process, as many physical ailments, such as cancer and arthritis, are directly related to accumulated anger and resentment.

2. Now write down everyone you can think of in your life who you feel you have hurt or done an injustice to, and write down what you did to these people.

    Again close your eyes, relax, and imagine each person in turn. Tell each one what you did, and ask the person to forgive you and give you his or her blessing. Then picture the person doing so.

    When you have finished the process, write at the bottom of your paper (or across the whole thing), "I forgive myself and absolve myself of all guilt, here and now, and forever!" Then tear up the paper and throw it away.

ONE FINAL CLEARING PROCESS

Go through your closets, drawers, basement, garage, or desk — wherever you have accumulated "stuff" that you don't need, and throw it out or give it away.

This vigorous, concrete action on the physical level is symbolic of what you are doing on mental, emotional, and psychic levels — clearing out old, useless stuff, getting the energy flow moving, and getting your "house in order." It will make you feel great, especially if you do affirmations while you're doing it, such as:

The more I outflow, the more space I create
for good things to come to me.

I love giving and I love receiving.

CLEARING

*As I clean up and clear out my physical space
I am cleaning up and clearing out my life in every way.*

*I am now putting my life in order, preparing to accept
all the good that is coming to me now.*

*I give thanks now for all the good that I have
and all the good things to come.*

WRITING AFFIRMATIONS

The technique I'm about to describe has brought some of the fastest and most dramatic changes in my life on many different occasions. It is a combination of writing affirmations and a clearing process, neatly rolled into one. I love it because it is so simple and easy to do, yet it gets down to a very deep level.

Writing affirmations is a very dynamic technique because the written word has so much power over our minds. We are both writing and reading them at the same time, so it's like a double hit of energy.

Take any affirmation you want to work with and write it ten or twenty times in succession on a piece of paper. Use your name, and try writing it in the first, second, and third persons. (For example: *I, John, am a successful singer and songwriter. John, you are a successful singer and songwriter. John is a successful singer and songwriter.*)

Don't just write it by rote; really think about the meaning of the words as you are writing them. Notice whether you feel any resistance, doubts, or negative thoughts about what you are writing. Whenever you do (even a slight one), turn the paper over, and on the back write out the negative thought, the reason why the affirmation can't be true, can't work, or whatever. (For example: *I'm really not good enough. I'm too old. This isn't going to work.*) Then go back to writing the affirmation.

When you are finished, take a look at the back of the paper. If you have been honest, you will have a good look at the reasons why you keep yourself from having what you want in this particular case.

With this in mind, think of some affirmations you can do to help you specifically counteract these negative fears or beliefs, and begin to write out these new affirmations. For example, if one of your negative beliefs is, "*I can't be more successful than my father was,*" you could affirm, "*My father is proud and happy about my success.*" Or you may want to stick with the original affirmation if it seems effective, or modify it slightly to be more accurate.

Keep working with writing the affirmations once or twice a day for a few days. Once you feel that you've really looked at your negative programming, discontinue writing it out, and just keep writing the affirmations.

My experience with this process is that often whatever I have been affirming manifests surprisingly quickly after going through the clearing process. And I have usually received many valuable insights into my own patterns this way.

SETTING GOALS

Possibly the trickiest part of getting what you want in life is just figuring out what you really want! And yet it is certainly the most important part of all.

In my own life I have found that once I have a clear, strong intention to create something, it often happens quickly and easily. I experience this as a kind of "click" in my consciousness, when I suddenly get a very strong experience of what I want, and an equally strong experience that I'm going to get it.... It usually takes a certain amount of time and energy spent in processing before I arrive at that point of clarity. And very often the "click of clarity" has been preceded by feelings of confusion, despair, hopelessness, and so on, which I have had to work my way through. So don't worry... the darkest hour is truly just before the dawn.

The most extreme example of this in my own life was the ten-year process of deep emotional healing that I went through in order to get clear about my intention to find my life partner. Although I thought I was ready for this to happen, I discovered that I had much deep fear and ambivalence. Once I was able to acknowledge these feelings consciously, and work with healing my fears and old emotional patterns, my intention became clear. Three weeks later, I got together with the man who is now my husband!

Discovering what you want in your life can be facilitated by the process of setting goals. I often find it helpful to do some exercises with pen and paper, which I share with you here. When you are working on setting goals it's important to keep a few things in mind.

Remember that setting goals does *not* mean that you are stuck with those goals. You can change them as often as you want to and feel that it's necessary.

Remember also that setting goals does not mean that you have to pursue them through excess effort, striving, or struggling. It does *not* mean that you have to become emotionally addicted to achieving them. On the contrary, setting goals can help you flow through life more easily, effortlessly, and pleasurably. The nature of life is movement and creativity, and goals give you a clear focus and direction in which to channel your natural creative energy. This helps you to outflow and contribute to the world, which enhances your feeling of well-being and satisfaction in life. Goals are there to help you and support you in your true purpose.

Goals can be made in the spirit that life is an enjoyable game to be played, and one that can be deeply rewarding. They are not to be taken too heavily or seriously. At the same time, you must give them enough weight and importance so they are of real value to you.

You may find that the very process of choosing goals brings up a certain amount of emotional resistance in you. You might experience this in various different ways, such as feeling depressed, hopeless, or overwhelmed at the thought of trying to set goals. Or you might feel the desire to distract yourself by eating, sleeping, or other activities. These emotional reactions (if you should have them) are clues to the ways in which you avoid getting what you want in life. It's important to go ahead and experience these feelings and reactions, to go through them, and proceed with the process. Once you get into it you will find it of value.

Then again, you may thoroughly enjoy the whole process and find it very expansive, fun, and enlightening. I hope so!

Don't make the choosing of goals too complicated or significant. Start with simple, obvious things. Remember you can always change and develop them as you go along.

EXERCISES

1. Sit down with a pen and paper and write down the following categories:

Personal growth/education

Work/career

Relationships

Creative self-expression

Money

Lifestyle/possessions

Leisure/travel

135

Now, keeping in mind your present life situation, write down under each category some things that you would like to have, to change, or to improve upon in the near future. Don't think too hard about it; simply write down any ideas that come to your mind as good possibilities.

The purpose of this exercise is to loosen you up and

get you thinking about what you want in the various areas of your life.

2. Take another piece of paper and write at the top: *"If I could be, do, and have everything I want, this would be my ideal scene."*

    Now list the same seven categories and, after each one, write a paragraph or two (or however much you want!) describing your absolute ideal situation in life, as far as you can fantasize about it.

    The purpose of this exercise is to stretch and expand you beyond your present limits, so let your imagination take over, and really let yourself have everything you could ever want.

    When you have finished this, add one more category — *World situation/environment*. Describe the kinds of changes you would like to see happen in the world in your lifetime, if you could have the power to change things — world peace, the end of poverty, people becoming conscious of one another and the earth, living in harmony with nature, schools transformed into exciting learning centers, hospitals becoming true centers of healing, and so on. You can be as creative as you like with this category, and you may find that you have all kinds of interesting ideas you never thought of before.

    Now reread the whole thing and meditate on it awhile. Create a mental picture for yourself of a wonderful life in a beautiful world.

3. Again, take a fresh sheet of paper. Based on what seems most meaningful from the ideal scene you have created above, write a list of the ten or twelve most important

goals for your life, as you feel them to be right now. Remember that you can change and revise this list at any time (and you should do so from time to time).

4. Now write down, "My Five-Year Goals," and list the most important goals you would like to achieve within the next five years.

It's great to write your goals in the form of affirmations, as if they have already been achieved. This helps to achieve a clearer, stronger effect. For example:

I now own and live on twenty acres of land in the country, with a beautiful house, orchards, a creek, and lots of animals.

I now support myself easily and abundantly through leading seminars and giving speeches to enthusiastic and appreciative audiences.

In writing your goals, be sure to put down things that are real and meaningful to you, things that you actually want, not what you think you should want. No one else need ever see your goals unless you want them to, and this process requires that you be totally honest with yourself.

5. Repeat the process above with your goals for one year. Don't make too many; if you have a lot at first, eliminate all but the five or six most important ones. Check to see that they are in alignment with your five-year goals. That is, make sure they are moving in the same general direction, so that when you accomplish your

one-year goals, you will be a step closer to your five-year goals. For example, if one of your five-year goals is to own your own business, one of your one-year goals might be to have a certain amount of money saved toward that end, or to have a job in a similar business where you are getting a certain type of experience you will need.

Now write out your goals for six months from now, one month, and one week from now. Again, keep it simple and choose the three or four that are most important to you. Be realistic about how much you can accomplish in the shorter-range goals. Again, make sure they are in alignment with your longer-range goals.

You may find it difficult to be so specific about events so far in the future, and you may have an uncomfortable feeling about planning ahead. However, just making a plan does not oblige you to follow it; in fact, you are bound to change considerably. This exercise is for the purpose of:

1. Getting practice in setting goals.

2. Acknowledging that some of your fantasies can become reality if you wish them to.

3. Getting in touch with some of the important purposes and directions in your life.

I suggest that you keep your goals in your notebook. Every now and then, perhaps every few months or so, or whenever it feels like a helpful thing to do, sit down with your notebook and do some of the processes again, revising and reshaping your goals as needed. Be sure to date your paper each time you do this, and keep your lists in order in your notebook, as it is very interesting and informative to look back and see how they gradually evolve.

SOME GENERAL RULES

1. For short-range goals (one week, one month) be fairly simple and realistic — choose things that you are pretty sure you can accomplish, unless you especially feel like taking on a big challenge (which can be very good sometimes). The more long-range your goal, the more expansive and imaginative you can be, so that your horizons are constantly extended.

2. When you find that you have not accomplished some of your goals (which will inevitably happen), do not criticize yourself or assume that you have failed. Simply acknowledge clearly to yourself that you have not accomplished that goal, and decide whether or not it is still a goal for you; that is, decide whether you want to set it again for yourself, or whether you want to let it go. It is *most* important that you acknowledge unaccomplished goals in this way. Otherwise, they may accumulate in the back of your mind and you will feel unconsciously that you have "failed," which will eventually make you tend to avoid the goal-setting process.

3. When you find that you *have* accomplished a goal, even a small one, be sure to acknowledge yourself for that. Give yourself a pat on the back and enjoy at least a

moment of satisfaction about it. All too often, we accomplish our goals and forget to even notice or enjoy the fact that we have done so!

4. Don't take on too much at once. Set goals that feel good to you. If you feel overwhelmed, confused, or discouraged . . . simplify. You may want to work on goals in one area of your life only, such as your job or your relationships. This process is ultimately to help you enjoy your life more.

If you set a lot of goals that you don't accomplish, you may be setting them unrealistically high, or setting goals that you don't truly desire and, therefore, have no real inner intention of pursuing. Choose goals that you genuinely like and want, and are realistic for you.

If you consistently feel blocked in pursuing or achieving your goals, you may have some unconscious patterns stopping you. I recommend finding a good therapist or support group to help you do some emotional healing work. We all need help and extra support at times.

Remember, too, that there is a time to set goals and a time to let them go. Just trust the flow of your life to get you where you need to go.

IDEAL SCENE

Creative visualization can take the form of mental imagery, of spoken or written words, or of a physical image or picture (see the next section on "treasure maps"). Anything that helps you to create a clear blueprint to put out in the universe is an aid in creative visualization.

This exercise helps you to create a clear picture through written words. The process of doing it helps you get clearer about what you really want, and it helps you to manifest it. I use it for all my important goals.

Think of a goal that is important to you. It can be a long-range or short-range one.

Write down the goal as clearly as possible in one sentence.

Underneath that, write, "Ideal Scene," and proceed to describe the situation exactly as you would like it to be when your goal is fully realized. Describe it in the present tense, as if it already exists, in as much detail as you wish.

When you have finished, write at the bottom, *"This, or something better, now manifests for me in totally satisfying and harmonious ways, for the highest good of all concerned,"* and add any other affirmations you wish, and sign your name.

Then sit quietly, relax, visualize your ideal scene at your meditative level of mind, and do your affirmations.

Keep your ideal scene in your notebook, in your desk, near your bed, or hang it on your wall. Read it often, and make appropriate changes when necessary. Bring it to mind during your meditation periods.

One word of warning... if you put it away in a drawer and forget about it, you are very likely to find one day that it has manifested anyhow... without your consciously putting any energy into it at all.

I have often looked back through my old goals, ideal scenes, and treasure maps, surprised to find that things I had completely forgotten about had magically come into being in my life.

TREASURE MAPS

Making a "treasure map" is a very powerful technique, and fun to do.

A treasure map is an actual, physical picture of your desired reality. It is valuable because it forms an especially clear, sharp image which can then attract and focus energy into your goal. It works along the same lines as a blueprint for a building.

You can make a treasure map by drawing or painting it, or by making a collage using pictures and words cut from magazines, books or cards, photographs, drawings, and so on. Don't worry if you're not artistically accomplished. Simple, childlike treasure maps are just as effective as great works of art!

Basically the treasure map should show you in your ideal scene, with your goal fully realized.

Here are some guidelines that will help you make the most effective treasure maps:

1. Create a treasure map for a single goal or area of your life, so that you can be sure to include all the elements without getting too complicated. This enables the mind to focus on it more clearly and easily than if you include all your goals on one treasure map. You might want to do one treasure map for your relationships, one for your job, one for your spiritual growth, and so on.

2. You can make it any size that's convenient for you. You may want to keep it in your notebook, hang it on your wall, or carry it in your pocket or purse. I usually make mine on light cardboard, which holds up better than paper.

3. Be sure to put yourself in the picture. For a very realistic effect, use a photograph of yourself. Otherwise draw yourself in. Show yourself being, doing, or having your desired objective — traveling around the world, wearing your new clothes, or being the proud author of your new book.

4. Show the situation in its ideal, complete form, as if it already exists. You don't need to indicate how it's going to come about. This is the finished product. Don't show anything negative or undesirable.

5. Use lots of color in your treasure map to increase the power and impact on your consciousness.

6. Show yourself in a real setting; make it look believable to yourself.

7. Include some symbol of the infinite which has meaning and power for you. It could be an om sign, a cross, Christ, Buddha, a sun radiating light, or anything that represents universal intelligence or God. This is an acknowledgment and a reminder that everything comes from the infinite source.

8. Put affirmations on your treasure map. *"Here I am driving my new hybrid gas and electric car."*
   Be sure to also include the cosmic affirmation, *"This, or something better, now manifests for me in totally satisfying and harmonious ways, for the highest good of all concerned."*

The process of creating your treasure map is a powerful step toward manifesting your goal. Now just spend a few minutes each day quietly looking at it, and every once in a while throughout the day give it a thought. That is all that's necessary.

SOME SAMPLE IDEAS FOR TREASURE MAPS

Here are a few possible ideas for treasure maps to stimulate your imagination:

HEALTH

Show yourself radiantly healthy, active, beautiful, participating in whatever activities would indicate perfect health.

WEIGHT OR PHYSICAL CONDITION

Show yourself with your perfect body, feeling wonderful about yourself (cut a picture from a magazine that looks like you would look in your perfect condition, and paste a photo of your head on the body!). You can make statements with balloons around them coming out of your mouth like in cartoons, to indicate how you are feeling, such as, "I feel wonderful and look fantastic now that I weigh 125 pounds and am in great physical condition."

SELF-IMAGE AND BEAUTY

Show yourself as you want to feel about yourself . . . beautiful, relaxed, enjoying life, warm and loving. Include words and symbols that represent these qualities to you.

RELATIONSHIPS

Put photos of yourself and your friend, lover, husband, wife, family member, or coworker in your treasure map, with pictures, symbols, and affirmations showing that you are happy, loving, communicating, enjoying a deep, wonderful sexual relationship, or whatever is appropriate and desirable for that relationship.

If you are looking for a new relationship, find pictures and words that represent qualities you desire in the person and the relationship; show yourself with the ideal person for you.

JOB OR CAREER

Show yourself doing what you really want to do, with interesting, agreeable coworkers, earning plenty of money (be specific about how much you want), in the location you desire, and any other pertinent details.

CREATIVITY

Use symbols, colors, and pictures that indicate your creativity is really opening up. Show yourself doing and manifesting creative, beautiful, interesting things and feeling great about them.

FAMILY AND FRIENDS

Show members of your family or friends in totally harmonious, loving relationships with you and each other.

TRAVEL

Show yourself wherever you want to be, with plenty of time and money to enjoy your location.

And so on. You get the idea. Have fun!

HEALTH AND BEAUTY

There are so many ways that creative visualization can be used to maintain and improve our health, physical fitness, and beauty. Like everything else, our health and attractiveness are created by our mental and emotional attitudes. So changing our beliefs and the way we tune into ourselves and the world can have profound physical effects.

I have already mentioned the value of doing treasure maps in these areas. Here are a few other techniques that I like to use. I'm sure you'll find many more of your own.

PHYSICAL EXERCISE

No matter what type of physical exercise you do, you can use creative visualization and affirmation to help you get the maximum amount of benefit and enjoyment from it. You can use visualization both while you are doing the physical exercise, and also at other times, while sitting in meditation or relaxing.

For example, if you like to run, picture yourself running very swiftly, smoothly, and tirelessly. While you are running, imagine that you are taking a huge leap with every step, covering vast territory effortlessly, almost flying. During relaxation periods, affirm to yourself that you are daily growing faster, stronger, and in better physical shape. Picture yourself winning races, if that is one of your goals.

If you do dance or yoga exercises, while you are doing them put your consciousness in your body, in your muscles; picture them relaxing and stretching, see yourself becoming more and more limber and flexible.

Use creative visualization to improve your abilities in your favorite sport; imagine yourself becoming more and more accomplished until you are truly excelling.

BEAUTY TREATMENTS

Do things for yourself regularly that make you feel like you are taking special care of yourself and doing nice things for your body. Using creative visualization can turn a daily routine into a beauty treatment ritual.

For example, take a hot bath or shower, and visualize the hot water totally relaxing, soothing, and healing you. Picture any problems melting or being washed away, and nothing remaining but your natural radiance, shining from within.

Put lotion or oil on your face and body, giving yourself lots of loving attention, affirming that your skin is becoming smoother and more beautiful all the time. When you wash your hair, put your attention on what you're doing, and affirm that your hair is thicker, shinier, and healthier than ever before. When you brush your teeth, mentally affirm that they are strong, healthy, and beautiful. And so on.

EATING RITUALS

Many people have negative concepts relating to food. We are afraid the food we eat is going to make us fat, or make us sick (unhealthy). Yet we tend to compulsively continue eating the very foods we fear, thus creating inner stress and conflict, and eventually creating the feared effects — overweight and illness.

Also, many people are not fully conscious while they eat. We are so busy talking and thinking of other things, we fail to tune in to the delicious, satisfying taste and nutrition of our food.

Eating is really a magic ritual, an amazing process in which various forms of energy from the universe are transformed into the energy that forms our bodies. Whatever we are thinking and feeling at the time is part of the alchemy.

Here is a ritual to practice at least once a day if possible, no matter what you are eating:

Sit down with your food in front of you. Close your eyes for a moment, relax, and take a deep breath. Silently thank the universe for this food, and thank all the beings who helped provide it, including the plants and animals, and the people who grew it and prepared it for you.

Open your eyes and look at the food; really observe what it looks like. Observe how it smells. Slowly begin to eat it; really be aware of and enjoy the taste. As you are eating, talk to yourself silently, and tell yourself that this food is being transformed into life energy for your use. Tell yourself that your body is using everything that it needs, and easily eliminating anything that it doesn't need. Picture yourself becoming healthier and more beautiful as a result of eating the food. Do this regardless of any other previous concepts you may have of how good or bad the food is for you.

If possible, eat slowly, stop when you feel satisfied, and take a moment or two after you finish to enjoy the pleasant warm glow that emanates from your stomach when it is satisfied and happy.

The more often you remember to tune into your food this way, the more beauty and good health you will create for yourself. Here is another ritual that is even simpler:

Before going to bed, when you arise, or sometime during the day, pour yourself a tall glass of cool water. Sit down, relax, and drink it slowly. As you drink, tell yourself that this water is the elixir of life and the fountain of youth. Imagine that it is washing away all impurities and bringing you energy, vitality, beauty, and health.

Here are some good affirmations for health and beauty:

Every day I am growing healthier and more attractive.

Everything I do adds to my health and beauty.

*Everything I eat adds to my health, beauty,
and attractiveness.*

I am good to my body, and my body is good to me.

I am now slender, strong, and in perfect condition no matter what I do.

I am growing stronger and more powerful every day.

I now desire to eat only those things that are best for me at any given time.

I get hungry only for the foods my body really needs.

The more I love and appreciate myself, the more beautiful I am becoming.

I am now irresistibly attractive to men (or women).

I love my body as it is.

I am naturally attractive as I am.

CREATIVE VISUALIZATION
IN GROUPS

Many of the techniques that I provide in this book can be easily adapted for use in groups. Creative visualization is especially good when used by a group, because the group energy automatically gives it a lot of power. Each person's energy tends to support the energy of others, and in this case the whole becomes more than the sum of its parts.

No matter what type of group you are involved in, whether it is your family or a group of friends, a work group, a social action group, a church or spiritual group, or a workshop or class, you may find that creative visualization provides you with tools for achieving your group's goals, or just for tuning into each other in a deeper way.

Here are some of the ways you can use creative visualization in a group:

SINGING AND CHANTING

Choose songs or chants that express a feeling, an idea, or an attitude that you want to create or cultivate in yourselves and in the world. Music is very powerful in effecting change.

MEDITATING AND IMAGING

Choose a goal or image, and have everyone sit in silent meditation, visualizing and affirming it together. You may be amazed at the results.

TREASURE MAPPING

Have each person create his or her own treasure map for a group goal, or as a group create one treasure map together. Or you can even appoint a committee to make a treasure map!

AFFIRMATIONS

Do affirmations in partners, as I describe in the section on how to use affirmations. Or have the whole group speak affirmations aloud together.

HEALING

Healing in groups is a wonderful experience. See the section on healing meditations.

CREATIVE VISUALIZATION
IN RELATIONSHIPS

One of the most valuable ways we can use creative visualization is in improving our relationships. Because human beings are so sensitive to each other on so many levels, we are especially susceptible and receptive to the thought forms that we hold about each other. It is these thought forms and the underlying attitudes that they reflect which form our relationships, and cause them to work or not work.

In a relationship, as in everything else, we get exactly what we believe in, expect, and "ask for" on our deepest levels. The people we are in relationships with are always a mirror, reflecting our own beliefs, and simultaneously we are mirrors, reflecting their beliefs. A relationship with another human being is one of the most powerful tools for growth that we have; if we look honestly at our relationships we can see so much about how we have created them.

Take an attitude of total responsibility about your relationship. Assume for a moment that you alone are responsible for creating it the way it is, no matter how much it may look to you like the other person is responsible for certain things. If there are certain things about the relationship that are unsatisfying to you, ask yourself why and how you have created it that way. Keep in mind, however, that taking responsibility for your life does not mean that you are *to blame* for the problems in your life or relationship.* See if you can discover what core beliefs you have that cause you to create a less than satisfying, happy, loving relationship. What is the payoff for you in keeping yourself in an unhappy space? (There is always a payoff in everything we do; otherwise we wouldn't do it.)

If you truly *desire* to have deeply fulfilling, happy relationships in your life, if you *believe* that it is possible for you to have them, and if you are willing to *accept* that happiness and satisfaction, then you can and will create relationships that work for you.

Here are some things you can do to help you with your relationships:

1. Look at your goals in the relationship. What do you truly want out of this relationship? Consider all levels — physical, emotional, mental, and spiritual. Write out an ideal scene, or do a treasure map that expresses your perfect visualization in this relationship.

2. Take a good honest look at what beliefs and attitudes are keeping you from creating what you want. You can use a clearing process to help you get in touch with your limiting attitudes. For example, you can write, "The reason I can't have a satisfying relationship with _____

---

* For clarification about the difference between responsibility and self-blame, read my book *The Path of Transformation*.

is...," or "The reason I can't have what I want in this relationship is...." Then write all the responses that come up for you.

3.   Use affirmations and visual imagery to change your negative beliefs, and to start visualizing and creating loving, fulfilling relationships.

4.   Use visualization to improve a difficult relationship. Let us say, for example, that you have difficulty getting along with someone and you would like to create a more harmonious relationship with that person:

After relaxing into a deep, quiet, meditative state of mind, imagine the two of you relating and communicating in an open, honest, and effective way. Imagine saying to this person anything you need to communicate in order to clear things up between you. Imagine the person listening and hearing you, then saying anything he or she needs to say, with you listening in return.

Repeat this exercise as needed. If you are sincere in your desire and intention, and open to change, you may find that the relationship is becoming easier and more flowing, and that the other person seems to become more agreeable and easier to communicate with. Eventually you may find that the problem will resolve itself completely, in one way or another, to the benefit of all parties concerned. This resolution may involve an actual communication with the person, or it may not.

5. The technique of saying affirmations to each other can often help to improve relationships dramatically. Of course it's very important to communicate with each other honestly from your true feelings about what you like and don't like, and what you want. But instead of continuously complaining about each other's short-comings and weaknesses, try making an agreement to affirm to each other that you are improving and making progress in your growth and development. So instead of, "George, why do you always interrupt me when I'm saying something?" you might agree to say to George at appropriate moments, "I appreciate the way you are becoming a good listener." In this way you not only remind George in a friendly way to be a better listener, but you also begin to change *your* image of George, as well as George's image of himself.

In ongoing relationships, all too often we have gotten stuck in certain roles and images with each other that we find difficult to change. It's as if we've put ourselves and each other in a certain box with certain labels on it. We find this very limiting and confining, but don't always know how to step out of it.

Creative visualization provides us with a helpful tool for expanding out of our roles and stereotypes. Begin to visualize and affirm new images for yourself and for the other person, see the potential for positive change within every person and every situation, and give energy and support to that positive change through creative visualization.

Remember, however, that human relationships are very complex. Our relationships perfectly reflect our own inner process; they are wonderfully effective mirrors to help us see the next step of our own growth. So if relationship difficulties persist, it is a message to us that a deeper level of our own healing is needed. I strongly recommend getting support from a good therapist or counselor who can help us see what the problems in our relationships are trying to teach us.

161

PART FIVE

Living Creatively

*The only successful manifestation
is one which brings about a change
or growth in consciousness;
that is, it has manifested God,
or revealed Him more fully,
as well as having manifested a form.*

— David Spangler, *Manifestation*

CREATIVE CONSCIOUSNESS

Creative visualization is not just a technique; ultimately it is a state of consciousness. It is a consciousness in which we deeply realize that we are the continuous creators of our universe, and we take responsibility for that in every moment.

There is no separation between us and God; we are divine expressions of the creative principle on this level of existence. There can be no real lack or scarcity; there is nothing we have to try to achieve or attract; we contain the potential for everything within us.

Manifestation through creative visualization is the process of realizing and making visible on the physical plane our divine potential.

DISCOVERING YOUR
HIGHER PURPOSE

A basic need of all human beings is to make a positive contribution to the world and to our fellow beings, as well as to improve and enjoy our personal lives. We all have a great deal to offer the world and to each other, each in our own special and unique way. To a great degree, our own personal sense of well-being is a function of how much we are expressing this.

We each have a significant contribution to make in this lifetime. It may involve many things, or it may be something very simple. I call this contribution our higher purpose. It always involves being yourself totally, completely, and naturally, and doing something or many things that you genuinely love to do, and that you have a natural gift for.

We all know in our hearts what our higher purpose is, but we often do not consciously acknowledge it, even to ourselves. In fact, most people seem to go to great lengths to hide it from themselves and from the world. They fear and seek to avoid the power, responsibility, and light that comes with acknowledging and expressing their true purpose in life.

As you use creative visualization, you will find that you become more and more attuned to and aware of your higher purpose. Notice the elements that tend to recur in your dreams, goals, and fantasies, the particular qualities that are there in the things you find yourself doing and creating. These are important clues to the underlying meaning and purpose of your life.

In using creative visualization, you will find that your ability to manifest will work to the degree that you are in alignment with your higher purpose. If you try to manifest something and it doesn't seem to work, it may not be appropriate to the underlying pattern and meaning of your life. Be patient and keep tuning into your inner guidance. In retrospect, you will see that everything is unfolding perfectly.

168

This is a time of great transformation on our planet. We all have a part to play, just by being willing to be our true, magnificent selves.

YOUR LIFE IS YOUR WORK OF ART

I like to think of myself as an artist, and my life is my greatest work of art. Every moment is a moment of creation, and each moment of creation contains infinite possibilities. I can do things the way I've always done them, or I can look at all the different alternatives, and try something new and different and potentially more rewarding. Every moment presents a new opportunity and a new decision.

What a wonderful game we are all playing, and what a magnificent art form....

ACKNOWLEDGMENTS

ORIGINAL ACKNOWLEDGMENTS, 1978

Thank you to Marc Allen and Dean Campbell for your love and support in writing this book and in all other ways. Thank you, Rainbow Canyon, for your beautiful friendship. And special thanks to my mother, Elizabeth, for all your love, wisdom, and encouragement.

I'd also like to thank all the incredible teachers who have contributed so much to my life and happiness, as well as to the understanding that has been channeled into this book. Some of you I have known as gurus, some I have known as personal friends and lovers, and others of you have come to me in the form of books. To all of you I send my love and appreciation.

Last but not least, I'd like to acknowledge and thank my own inner guidance that keeps showing me the way... reminding me how beautiful life really is... and that actually is responsible for writing this book.

ACKNOWLEDGMENTS, 2008

Since this book was originally published in 1978, many people have contributed to my life and helped me develop my work. To all of you, thank you! I would like to especially thank Drs. Hal and Sidra Stone, my teachers, mentors, and close friends.

Thank you to Marc Allen, who has continued to support and encourage my creativity. Thanks to the entire New World Library staff for your contributions to my books and for carrying the message of personal growth through your publishing work.

A very special and heartfelt thank you to my dear friend and manager, Gina Vucci Long — without you I would not be able to do what I do. Thank you, Jim Burns, my loving husband, for all your patience and support.

RECOMMENDED RESOURCES

BOOKS AND AUDIOS BY SHAKTI GAWAIN AVAILABLE FROM NATARAJ PUBLISHING/ NEW WORLD LIBRARY

Awakening: A Daily Guide to Conscious Living (revised edition, 2006). 365 entries that offer a bit of Shakti's wisdom to ponder for each day.

Creating True Prosperity (1997). Here Shakti presents a new definition of prosperity, one that places importance on fulfillment of the heart and soul rather than simply on monetary gain.

Creative Visualization CD (1995). The unabridged audio version, read by the author on two CDs.

The Creative Visualization Workbook (1982). A large-format book, especially designed to accompany *Creative Visualization*, leads us step-by-step in planning our goals.

Developing Intuition: Practical Guidance for Daily Life (2000). Clear, practical advice and simple exercises that show us how to develop our intuitive ability.

Developing Intuition CD (2000). The unabridged audio version, read by the author on three CDs.

The Four Levels of Healing: A Guide to Balancing the Spiritual, Mental, Emotional, and Physical Aspects of Life (1997). Shakti's insights on identifying, balancing, and integrating all four levels of existence.

Living in the Light: A Guide to Personal and Planetary Transformation (with Laurel King; 1998). Practical guidance on developing our intuition and learning to follow it on a daily basis.

Meditations: Creative Visualization and Meditation Exercises to Enrich Your Life (1991). An easy-to-implement approach to finding and following inner wisdom, through eleven guided meditations on specific topics based on Shakti's workshops and writing.

Meditations CD (1989). Shakti leads four of her most powerful guided meditations: Contacting Your Inner Guide, The Male and Female Within, Discovering Your Inner Child, and Expressing Your Creative Being.

The Path of Transformation: How Healing Ourselves Can Change the World (revised edition, 2000). This book gives us the tools for healing ourselves on all levels — spiritually, mentally, emotionally, and physically, and shows that as we heal ourselves, we transform the world.

Reflections in the Light: Daily Thoughts and Affirmations (revised edition, 2003). A book of daily insights and affirmations.

BOOKS AND AUDIOS BY OTHER AUTHORS

Embracing Each Other by Dr. Hal Stone and Dr. Sidra Stone (Delos, Inc., 1989). A fascinating book that shows us exactly how our relationships mirror our own inner processes and can therefore be our best teachers.

Embracing Our Selves by Dr. Hal Stone and Dr. Sidra Stone (Nataraj Publishing/New World Library, 1989). This brilliant book shows us the many different "selves" within us and how we can integrate them to find balance and harmony.

Embracing Your Inner Critic by Dr. Hal Stone and Dr. Sidra Stone (HarperSanFrancisco, 1992). Gives practical help for effectively dealing with self-criticism.

Healing Words: The Power of Prayer and the Practice of Medicine by Larry Dossey, MD (HarperSanFrancisco, 1994). A medical doctor discusses modern research supporting the effectiveness of prayer and visualization.

Kinship with All Life by J. Allen Boone (HarperSanFrancisco, 1994). A unique and beautiful book. Although primarily concerned with human relationships with animals, it contains deep wisdom and insight about the use of visualization and affirmation in all relationships.

Meet Your Inner Critic CD or audiotape by Dr. Hal Stone and Dr. Sidra Stone (Delos, Inc., 1990). Further help for dealing with the inner critic.

The Nature of Personal Reality (A Seth Book) by Jane Roberts (New World Library/Amber Allen Publishing, 1994). An excellent explanation of how we are each totally responsible for creating our own reality.

174

ABOUT THE AUTHOR

Shakti Gawain is the bestselling author of *Creative Visualization, Living in the Light, The Path of Transformation, Creating True Prosperity, Developing Intuition,* and several other books. A warm, articulate, and inspiring teacher, Shakti leads workshops internationally. For more than thirty years, she has facilitated thousands of people in learning to trust and act on their own inner truth, thus releasing and developing their creativity in every area of their lives.

Shakti and her husband, Jim Burns, make their home in Mill Valley, California.